Risk Factors

Risk Factors and Business Models

Understanding the Five Forces of Entrepreneurial Risk and the Causes of Business Failure

D. Anthony Miles

DISSERTATION.COM

Boca Raton

Risk Factors and Business Models:
Understanding the Five Forces of Entrepreneurial Risk and the
Causes of Business Failure

Dissertation.com
Boca Raton, Florida
USA • 2011

ISBN-10: 1-59942-388-X
ISBN-13: 978-1-59942-388-3

Cover photo @Cutcaster.com/Adrian Grosu

Abstract

One of the primary concerns in a small business is the problem of risk. Many who begin the start-up process terminate it in less than one year. Of those that survive, many are unable to achieve sustained growth and profits. Small-to-medium business enterprises (SME) have a 50% to 90% chance of failure within the first five years. While there are measures of personal risk behavior of entrepreneurs, the literature contains no measure of risk orientation for the enterprise.

The purpose of this study was to develop and validate a researcher-designed instrument to measure the critical forces of business risk. The 37-item Entrepreneurial Risk Assessment Scale (ERAS) was developed from key theoretical concepts grounded in economics, marketing, management, finance, and entrepreneurship literature. It was developed and finalized through a process of reviewing literature, subject matter expert panels' review, and a pilot test. The a priori assumption of the ERAS constructs were (a) personal characteristics, (b) intangible operations, (c) enterprise operations, (d) market climate, and (e) business environment.

This study utilized a quantitative methodology to establish construct, content, and criterion validity using Bryant's (2000) framework found in *Reading and Understanding More Multivariate Statistics* edited by Grimm and Yarnold (2000). A sample ($N = 276$) was taken from an urban/suburban area in South Texas. A principal axis factoring (PAF) analysis was used to establish construct validity; a principle component analysis (PCA) was used to establish content validity; and a logistic regression was used to establish criterion validity. Reliability was assessed within the efforts to establish content validity.

What emerged from both the factor analyses were five new factors of entrepreneurial risk that were different from the a priori assumptions and thus renamed: (a) customer and resources, (b) security, (c) operations, (d) external pressures, and (e) other/alternate factors. The results of the PAF and PCA provided strong support for the content and construct validity of the ERAS instrument. In the assessment of criterion validity, the logistic regression analysis showed the endogenous factors, (a) customer and resources, and (c) operations reliably predicted risk behavior of both nascent and incumbent SMEs.

Acknowledgements

I wish to acknowledge several great individuals who have supported me in this endeavor:

First very special thanks to my mother and mentor, Bettye L. Miles, for her undying support, love and guidance.

Very special thanks to my brother Kevin Miles, who is following my footsteps with the goal of attaining a doctorate.

Very special thanks to my beautiful daughters, Jada and Andrea Miles and their mother, Charla Hudgins.

Very special thanks to all the Miles Family members for their undying support, love, and faith.

Very special thanks to my Uncle Ralph Miles, who is a great mentor, motivator, and the statistician of the family.

Very special thanks to my mentor, Mrs. Lillie Wilson Harris, who believed in me and instilled in me great wisdom and vision.

Very special thanks: it is with great pleasure to honor my dissertation Chair, Dr. Denise Staudt, who has not only been a great mentor and teacher, but also a great role model whose influence has pushed me to be a better researcher and scholar.

Very special thanks to Dr. Kevin Vichcales and Dr. Denise Doyle for their guidance, counsel, intervention, and tremendous support throughout this endeavor despite significant obstacles.

Very special thanks to my dissertation committee members for their fantastic encouragement and outstanding support: Dr. Richard Gray, Dr. David Vequist and Dr. Nursen Zanca whose advice, suggestions and comments helped to make this study possible.

Very special thanks to my mentor, Dr. Jack Davis, who made me a better researcher and scholar.

Very special thanks to my advisor, Dr. Frances Musa Boakari who made me a better writer and scholar.

Very special thanks to my mentor, Dr. Luisa Urdaneta who was my professor at University of Texas at San Antonio and inspired and taught me the science of anthropology.

I would be remiss if I did not mention the assistance of coworkers, professional colleagues, students, and friends at Texas A&M University, Palo Alto College, University of the Incarnate Word, Our Lady of the Lake University, Webster University, St. Mary's University, and University of Texas at San Antonio.

I am extremely grateful and greatly indebted to the individuals and organizations that assisted me with my pilot and formal study: Ms. Diana Cruz, the Westside Chamber of Commerce; Al Salgado, Orestes Hubbard, Mike Reyes and David Baesinger of UTSA's Small Business Development Center (SBDC); Cindy Solano and Pamela Sapia of the Small Business Administration (SBA); Gwendolyn Robinson, Alamo Black City Chamber; Bexar County Small Business Department; Hugo Villarreal, City of San Antonio Economic Development Department; Dr. Dave Palmer, SCORE; Estella Forhan, YWCA SEED Program; and Raul Rodriguez, University of the Incarnate Word.

Very special thanks to the hundreds of SMEs who were willing to participate in this study. I hope that my findings will be beneficial to you.

Very special thanks to: Mr. Eddie Harris of St. Philips College for his words of encouragement and mentorship in this endeavor.

Very special thanks to someone special: Dr. L'Nea Stewart for her words of encouragement and support in this endeavor.

Lastly, very special thanks to those people who helped and supported me that I forgot to mention.

All praises due to Allah, the beneficent, the merciful for all praises are due forever…

Special Page of Acknowledgements

This section of this dissertation is dedicated to the people that were part of my journey and who are no longer here to share my accomplishment. I wish to acknowledge the following persons in chronological order who have been a key ingredient and special influence in this endeavor of your passing:

First, this dissertation is dedicated to my late father, Winston C. Miles. My father had enough foresight and made me go to college when I was 18 years and hated school. My father preached education. My father believed in me and said I can do anything if I put my mind to it. This was contrary to a high school counselor telling me I was not college material. My father often said to me, "Failure is not an option. Your younger brothers and sisters are watching you. Failure is unacceptable." My father also taught me the value of a work ethic and made me get a job to put myself through college. My father was the trailblazer and the first person in the Miles Family to graduate from college at St. Mary's University. Because of your words of wisdom, I do not have the luxury of entertaining the thought of failure. For all the obstacles and racism that you endured, you would not accept anything less than excellence from your children. I hope that one day I can at least approach the shoelaces of your greatness. I miss you dearly.

To Dr. Reginald Traylor, I want to thank you for being my mentor and teacher. You were the first professor that I took courses from at the University of the Incarnate Word. The last time I saw you we were both attending a conference in Utah. I have learned so much from you and your brilliant mind. I still cannot believe that you are gone.

To my grandmother, Mrs. Alice Davis, you were and still are a huge part of my life. You are such an inspiration to me. I am still not over your passing. It was one of the most difficult tragedies in my life. Without your support, I do not know how I would have reached this accomplishment. You meant so much to me in my life. Our family is still trying to carry on your spirit in our hearts. I miss you dearly. You were the rock in our family.

To my uncle/friend, Timothy Miles, it is so difficult to accept that you are no longer with us. You left before your time. It is not the same since you have left us. Thank you so much for being supportive in my endeavor. I cannot count the number of days that our family misses your colorful presence. We miss you immensely. Take care.

To my uncle, Joseph Miles ("Uncle Joe"), we miss you and your lively spirit. Your passing this year saddened us all. We hope that you are smiling down on us from the heavens. Thank you for being supportive in my endeavor. It just will not be the same without you. The Miles Family really misses you. Take care.

Lastly, I want to thank my uncle, Sam Weddington. Our family continues to be affected by your passing. Every day I am constantly reminded of your absence. You were the celebrity of the family appearing in the two "Ace Ventura" movies with Jim Carrey. I miss your laugh and your strength. I have learned so much from you. I wish that I had your gift of patience and forgiveness. I want to thank you for being a loyal son and for being the great man who took care of my grandmother. I am so indebted to you.

Table of Contents

List of Tables

List of Figures

List of Abbreviations

BET	Black Entertainment Television
BPEA	Business Plan Evaluation Aids
CD	Compact Disk
CFA	Confirmatory Factory Analysis
DOS	Diseconomies of Scale
EFA	Exploratory Factory Analysis
EO	Entrepreneurial Orientation
ER	Entrepreneurial Risk
ERAS	Entrepreneurial Risk Assessment Scale
ERO	Entrepreneurial Risk Orientation Behavior
FA	Factor Analysis
IRB	Institutional Review Board
KMO	Kaiser-Meyer-Olkin Measure
LLC	Limited Liability Corporation
LLP	Limited Liability Partnership
NAIC	North American Classification System
PAF	Principle Axis Factoring
PCA	Principle Component Analysis
ROI	Return on Investment
SAS	Statistical Analysis System ®
SBA	Small Business Administration
SBDC	Small Business Development Center
SEM	Structural Equation Modeling
SME	Small-to-Medium Business Enterprise
SPSS	Statistical Package for Social Sciences®
SSL	Sum of Squared Loadings
UIW	University of the Incarnate Word
USASBE	United States Association for Small Business and Entrepreneurship

List of Variables

AGE	Age
BCL	Business Climate/Economic Location
BET	Business Entity Type
CIR	Capital Investment Intensity
CMP	Competition Intensity
CTO	Customer Turnover/Turnaround
DSI	Diseconomies of Scale/Internet
EDU	Education
ENC	Environmental Climate
EOS	Equipment/Systems Investment
ETH	Ethnicity
EXI	Expertise in Industry/Field
GND	Gender
GLB	Globalization Risk
GRC	Government Regulation Constraints
INC	Income
IFC	Inflation/Energy/Fuel Costs
INT	Intellectual Capital
LBO	Length of Business Ownership
MEB	Market Entry/Exit Barriers
MPR	Market Potential
PMF	Protection Mechanisms
SCR	Security Risks
SRB	Social Responsibility
SRF	Social Risks
TRF	Terrorism Risks
TDP	Time Intensity Dependence
VOP	Velocity of Profit

Chapter 1

Introduction

The rate of survival for small-to-medium business enterprises has been and continues to be a challenging issue. A major problem with the pursuit of business ownership or entrepreneurship is the significant risks that are involved (Stanley & Danko, 1996). The problem is the high rate of failure of small-to-medium business enterprises (SME) and the often-ignored risk factors that act as strong antecedents. By nature, all businesses are risky; one's capacity to assume those risks is the defining concept of entrepreneurship (Cantillon, 1732/2001; Kanbur, 1982). Entrepreneurship is the polar opposite of safety and the two do not mix.

The Small Business Administration (SBA) defines a small-to-medium business enterprise (SME) as a business that has less than 500 employees (SBA Advocacy, 2007). "Entrepreneurial risk" (ER) is operationalized as "the risks that are associated with the success or failure of a business enterprise" (Ahwireng-Obeng & Mokgohlwa, 2002, p. 33). The economics literature states there are two general subcategories within the concept of entrepreneurial risk: (a) *endogenous variables*, factors controlled within the firm such as price, advertising, and operations; and (b) *exogenous variables*, factors outside the control of the firm such as consumer incomes, competitor prices and the weather (Dollinger, 1999; Hirschey, 2006; Hirschey & Pappas, 1992).

Background of the Study

The inspiration for conducting this study was the 2006 United States Association for Small Business and Entrepreneurship (USASBE) Conference in Tucson, Arizona. The researcher had the opportunity to present the topic as a workshop on a related subject concerning entrepreneurial risk metrics and measurement. The USASBE Conference provided the researcher an impetus to pursue this subject matter further as a research study. During the question and answer period following of the presentation, a few of the researchers in the audience stated how much they enjoyed the presentation on the subject of entrepreneurial risk measurement. After the positive responses received from the presentation at the conference, the researcher decided this subject needed more exploration; and would make an interesting dissertation topic for research.

Notably, a remarkably large percentage of people who begin the start-up process terminate it less than one year later (Shane, 2008). The SBA Office of Advocacy's general rule of thumb is that a new employer business has a 50% chance of surviving five years or more (Headd, 2003). The Small Business

Administration's (2005) statistics on small business failure report while 66% of new employer establishments survive at least two years, fewer than 50% survive to four years. Some of the research states that small-to-medium business enterprises (SMEs) have only a 10% chance of surviving in the first five years (Bee, 2004; Shane, 2008). They all agree that the typical entrepreneur forms a business that is gone within five years (Bee, 2004; Cressy, 2006; Eggers, 1999; Everett & Watson, 1998; Jarillo-Mossi, 1986; Stanley, 2001).

Numerous studies have concluded that financial vulnerability is a strong indicator of entrepreneurial failure (Beaver, 1966; Bernstein, 1990; Fitzpatrick, 1931). Gutter and Saleem's (2005) study concluded that financial vulnerability with SMEs could be determined by the extent to which income and wealth are derived from the same source. Economic factors appeared to have attributed to 30% to 50% of small business failures (Everett & Watson, 1998).

Other studies have attributed additional reasons why SMEs fail. Notably, Gaskill, Van Auken, and Manning (1993) and Osborne (1993) argued the reasons for entrepreneurial failure occurred due to: (a) undercapitalization, (b) poor planning, (c) lack of expertise and credibility, (d) poor money management, (e) failure to follow regulations with government entities, and (f) lack of managerial skill. Many entrepreneurs are great at creating dazzling plans however they fail in the implementation and management of people.

Other studies offered other considerations as to why SMEs fail. Beaver (1966) found that financial ratios proved useful in the prediction of bankruptcy and bond default at least five years before such situations actually occur. Amit, Glosten, and Muller (1993) concluded that by applying analytical, empirical, and experimental tools from a range of fields, some of the fundamental questions on small business success or failure could be answered. Everett and Watson (1998) concluded economic factors appear to be a factor in 30% to 50% of small business failures (e.g. lagging employment rates, interest rates, and others).

Many entrepreneurs start businesses in particular industries that are not best suited for startup ventures. As a result, certain factors influence success or failure. Those factors that influence success or failure are: *industry type and industry choice* (Gaskill, Van Auken, & Manning, 1993; Ricketts, Gaskill, Van Auken & Manning, 1993; Strotmann, 2007), *intangible forces* (management), *low market entry barriers* (Shane, 2008), *technology* (Abdelsamad & Kindling, 1978; Menefee & Parnell, 2007; Porter, 1998), *capitalization* (Watson & Everett, 1996) , *economic factors* (Parsa, Self, Njite, & King, 2005) and *market saturation dynamics* (Amit, Glosten, & Muller, 1993; Shane, 2008).

There are also issues concerning many entrepreneurs' lack of knowledge concerning the probability of success. By selecting the wrong business, significant risk often results in failure (Stanley, 2001). Businetz (1999) examined entrepreneurial biases and modes of behavior concerning the perception of risk and behavior. There have been other studies that have focused on entrepreneur risk perception (Anthony & Govindarajan, 2001; Murphy, Liao, & Welsch, 2006; Sherman, 2004; Yamada, 2004).

Since the very nature of entrepreneurship is centered upon risk and risk-taking, it raises the question as to why entrepreneurial risk has not warranted more research as a concept. Stanley (2001) argues there is a positive correlation between high risk and failure of a small business. Entrepreneurship is still a relatively new field of study in many university business programs. As such, more research is needed in the field of entrepreneurship.

This new interest in entrepreneurial studies has flourished in the current economy and is referred to as the "Information Age" (Bridges, 1994; Kiyosaki & Lechter, 1999). There is a movement toward less reliance on human capital (human labor) and more on information-based capital (automation). The paradigm shift from the industrial-based economy to an information-based economy has had an important influence on the employment sector through the corporate practices of downsizing and job elimination.

A major contributing factor to the gradual paradigm shift from the industrial-based economy to the information-based economy is the elimination of human labor-dependent functions: jobs. The information-based economy is a striking contrast to its predecessor, industrial-based economy. This contrast has been attributed to major corporations' ability to substitute information for human labor as a production resource (McInerney & White, 2000). Because of this paradigm shift, many individuals are considering entrepreneurship as a career alternative. The downside of this emerging trend of entrepreneurialism is the problem of risk: entrepreneurial risk.

Due to this paradigm shift, interest in entrepreneurship and self-employment has emerged. Under the pressure of the "dejobbing" of American companies, more people than ever before are starting their own businesses (Bridges, 1994). However, the downturn in the U.S. economy in 2008 has made it difficult to start a business enterprise. The effects from this are stronger in manufacturing industries as opposed to other industries such as sales and financial services (Shane, 2008). Fox (2009) declared that this is probably one of the worst times to start a business in this economy.

As a new emerging field of study, entrepreneurship continues to develop with new findings from the significant and vital scholarly research. The interest in entrepreneurship had strong emergence in the 1990's. A significant number of the prior studies focused chiefly on the risk aversive personality and risk-taking behaviors of the entrepreneur. The noted researchers in this area were Choi (2001), Da Silva (2000), Krueger (1998), Kuratko, Ireland, and Hornsby (2001), Littunen (2000), Rodriguez (2000), Vella (2001), and Wu & Knott (2005). There have been many studies on firm performance and reaction to risk from Foreman-Peck, Makepeace, and Morgan (2006), Martín, Sotos, & Picazo (2007), Hunter (2005), Leyden and Link (2004), and Sandino (2007).

3

What appears to be lacking from the prior studies is the focus on actually assessing the risk propensities of the business enterprise. From the prior studies, it became intriguing to examine the area of risk concerning small business enterprises. In addition, enterprise risk is an under-researched concept of entrepreneurship. A measure of enterprise risk orientation in businesses is needed to facilitate research in this area. This will be the central focus of this study.

Statement of the Problem

The risks involved with starting and maintaining a business enterprise are considerable. The major problems with the pursuit of entrepreneurship are the significant forces of risk that are involved. Entrepreneurial risk (ER) has been and continues to be a significant problem with nascent and incumbent small-to-medium business enterprises (SMEs). Considering SMEs have 50% to 90% chance of failure within the first five years (Bee, 2003; Headd, 2003; Shane, 2008), those significant forces of risks involved with entrepreneurship need to be examined.

The problem recognized as a basis for this study are the high rates of failures in SMEs calling for a significant investigation into the risk assessment of enterprises. Development of an instrument that contributes to that assessment will enable further research in the field of study.

Purpose of the Study

The purpose of this study is to develop and test an instrument to measure the critical forces of entrepreneurial risk. Building on key theoretical concepts grounded in economics, management, marketing, finance, and entrepreneurship literature, the Entrepreneurial Risk Assessment Scale (ERAS) is presented for measuring the risk forces associated with SMEs. The following research question(s) are addressed in this study:

1. Does the Entrepreneurial Risk Assessment Scale (ERAS) provide evidence of adequate instrument validity?

2. Does ERAS provide evidence of adequate instrument reliability?

Significance of the Study

The importance of this research is fourfold. This research attempts to: (a) develop an instrument to measure ER; (b) make a contribution to the theoretical understanding of ER as a construct, and contribute to the emerging entrepreneurship theory on risk and enterprise; (c) expand the prior research scope on entrepreneurial risk behavior by also examining the risk orientation and risk of the small-to-medium business enterprise; and (d) better understand the complexities of entrepreneurial risk.

Methodology

The study utilizes a quantitative approach using a sample of 276 small -to-medium enterprises (SME) from an estimated population of 25,000 of SMEs in an urban and suburban area. The researcher-developed Entrepreneurial Risk Assessment Scale (ERAS), which allows for examining characteristics of entrepreneurial risk in SMEs is validated following Bryant's (2000) data analysis strategies for establishing validity (construct, content, and criterion). Reliability will be assessed to establish content validity. Principal Axis Factoring (PAF) is used to established construct validity. Principal Component Analysis (PCA) is used to establish content validity. Logistic regression is used to establish criterion validity.

Assumptions of the Study

There are some assumptions concerning this study that will be acknowledged. The following assumptions serve as the basis for conducting this study:

1. The participants responded truthfully to the survey instrument. The researcher made the assumption that the responses to the questions are true. The data collected will be assumed to be as truthful and accurate as a possible;

2. The responses received from the survey were accurately interpreted.

3. A representative sample from the population was taken.

4. Differences between nascent and incumbent enterprises are indicators of entrepreneurial risk.

Delimitations of the Study

The study was delimited by certain conditions that were identified for this research inquiry. The scope of the study was delimited by the following conditions:

1. Geographical region. The study was confined to the San Antonio (Bexar County, Texas) area. The results may not be generally applicable to other geographic regions.

2. Population scope. The study was confined to small-to-medium business enterprises (SME) as the target population of this study in the San Antonio (Bexar County, Texas) area.

3. Sampling frame. The study confined itself to using a random sample, systematic random sample, and a convenience sample.

4. Population sample. The study was confined to a population of 25,456. A population sample of 276 SMEs recruited from the target area participants; the San Antonio (Bexar County, Texas).

5. Instruments used. The study was confined to using a 37-item Entrepreneurial Risk Assessment Scale (ERAS) instrument. The study was confined to examining subject matter found in the literature and reflected in the instrument.

6. Research design. This was confined to a cross-sectional non-experimental study.

7. Methodology. This study was confined to a quantitative methodology.

Definition of Terms

The concept of *entrepreneurial risk* is defined by Ahwireng-Obeng and Mokgohlwa (2002), "as the risks associated with the success or failure of a business enterprise" (p. 57). *Small-to-medium business enterprises* (SME) have three classifications: firms with less than 10 employees are defined as 'micro'; firms with less than 100 employees are defined as "small"; and firms with less than 500 employees are defined as 'medium'" (SBA, 2007). The term SME applies to all these classifications in this study.

This study examined entrepreneurial risk factors based on the dimensions of risk identified in the literature. The risks factors examined for this study are inclusive of both endogenous and exogenous. Table 1 illustrates the terms for entrepreneurial risk used for this study.

Table 1. Definition of Terms

Terms	Definitions
Personal Characteristics risks	Risks concerned with personal characteristics of the entrepreneur such as (a) age, (b) gender, (c) education, (d) ethnicity, (e) length of business ownership, (f) expertise in industry/field and (g) income.
Intangible Operation risks	Risks that are intangible influences to the business enterprise: (a) business entity type, (b) capital investment intensity, and (c) and time intensity dependence.
Enterprise Operations risks	Risks that are a major influence on the operations of the business enterprise: (a) labor/operating costs, (b) equipment/systems investment, (c) diseconomies of scale/ Internet, (d) protection mechanisms, (e) intellectual capital, (f) velocity of profit, (g) and customer turnover/turnaround.
Market Climate risks	Risks that are a major influence on the business enterprise with concerns for the market climate: (a) market potential, (b) market entry/exit barriers, (c) competition intensiveness, (d) business climate/ economic location, (e), government regulation constraints, and (f) social responsibility and (g) social risks.
Business Environment risks	Risks that are a major influence to the business enterprise in terms of the environment and its effect on profitability: (a) environmental climate, (b) security risk, (c) terrorism risk, (c) inflation/energy/fuel costs, and (d) globalization risk.

Summary of Chapter 1

The study is based on the fact that a large percentage of people who begin new businesses terminate them less than one year later (Bee, 2003; Shane, 2008). The purpose of the study is to develop and validate, a measure of entrepreneurial risk using Bryant's (2000) framework for validation. Assumptions, limitations, and definitions are provided. In the next chapter, the literature review covers the research and theory relevant to entrepreneurial risk as used to develop the Entrepreneurial Risk Assessment Scale (ERAS) instrument.

Chapter 2

Literature Review

This literature review discusses previous studies to illustrate the early development of entrepreneurial risk theory and establish the theoretical basis for the researcher-designed instrument. The first section of the review focuses on the classification of risk, business risk, financial risk, and global risk. The second section focuses on the theoretical framework directly related to the development of the Entrepreneurial Risk Assessment Scale (ERAS). The final section of the review summarizes the literature review sources for the development of the instrument.

Prior studies on entrepreneurial risk tended to focus on the behavior of entrepreneurs. There were many notable studies on risk tolerance and risk aversion behavior; the most important studies were referenced from Barbosa (1992), Bhide (1999a), and Businetz (1999). Later significant studies on risk aversion were from Declich and Ventura (2003), Rampini (2004), Gilmore, Carson, and O'Donnell (2004), and Xu and Ruef (2004). There were significant studies on risk personality behavior of entrepreneurs. Those studies were from Kanbur (1982), Mossi (1986), and Iyigun and Owen (1998). The most recent studies on risk personality behavior were from Da Silva (2000), Choi (2001), Diacon (2002), and Fritz (2006).

Some of the prior studies primarily focused on entrepreneur behavioral traits. Those studies were from Clouse (1986), Gallik (1989), and Askim (1999). The most recent studies on entrepreneur behavioral traits were from Da Silva (2000), Vella (2001), Davies, Hides, and Powell (2002), Hildebrando (2003), Stewart, Carland, Carland, Watson, and Sweo (2003), and Leyden and Link (2004).

Some of the important earlier studies that focused on risk propensity behavior were from Kanbur (1982), and Taylor (1992). Recent studies on risk propensity were from Da Silva (2000), Wu and Knotts (2005), Clemens & Heinemann (2006), and Norton & Moore (2002), and Norton and Moore (2006). Other studies referenced have focused on the effect of success or failure on the entrepreneur's behavior. Those studies were from Kuratko, Hornsby, and Naffzier (1997), Harting (2005), and Knott and Posen (2005). Krueger's (1998) study focused on risk assessment behavior of entrepreneurs. The more recent studies on risk assessment behavior were from Norton and Moore (2000), Sherman (2004), and Berglund (2005).

Drucker (1985) operationally defined "entrepreneurial" as a behavior by which established firms exploit new opportunities by entering new markets and sectors; and exploiting opportunities to expand their products/services to new markets. "Entrepreneurial risk" (ER) is operationalized as "the risks that are associated with the success or failure of a business enterprise" (Ahwireng-Obeng & Mokgohlwa, 2002, p. 33).

Classifications of Risk

Risk, as a concept, is defined as "the probability of loss" (Merriam-Webster, 1984). Different classifications of risk have been used in business and non-business sectors. The operational definition of *business risk* (also called operating risk) is defined as, "representing the underlying risk of the firm's operations in the absence of financing" (Hirschey, 2006, p. 133). Business risk can also be defined as the chance of loss associated with a given managerial decision (Hirschey, 2006). Gilmore, Carson, and O'Donnell (2004) theorized that risk could be defined as, "the likelihood that a new venture will fail to reach a satisfactory sales, profit, or return-on-investment (ROI)" (p. 15).

There are generally two types of business risk: *systematic* and *non-systematic.* Systematic risk (economy-based risk) includes factors that are firm specific and the risk level is rewarded. Non-systematic risk (firm or industry-based risk) includes factors that are common across a wide spectrum of firms. This risk is not rewarded because of risk limiting diversification strategies (Dollinger, 2002; White, Sondhi, & Fried, 1998).

Dickson and Giglierano (1986) distinguish between two types of entrepreneurial risk: (a) *sinking-the-boat risk*; which is the risk that a new venture will fail; and (b) *missing-the-boat risk,* which is the risk of missing out on a strategic opportunity. They noted, although the concept of risk is dominant in entrepreneurship literature, it is only the risk that a new venture will fail that is generally investigated.

For entrepreneurial risk, *downside risk* is defined as, "how much the venture can lose if it fails and how likely it is to fail" (Vesper, 1989, p. 149). Risks are described as two general types:

- *Endogenous risks* are controllable risks that are internal to the firm (Hirschey & Pappas, 1992; Laming & Kuehl, 2007; McCauly, 1986). These risks cannot necessarily be prevented, but purchasing insurance can minimize the financial loss. Examples are risk of fire, vandalism, and weather damage. These risks are also called *speculative risk* (Gahin, 1967; Megginson, Byrd, & Megginson, 2003).

- *Exogenous risks* are uncontrollable risks that are external to the firm (Hirschey & Pappas, 1992; Lambing & Kuehl, 2007; McAuley, 1986; Megginson et al., 2003). These risks have detrimental and financial impact, but cannot be covered by insurance. Examples are a new competitor locating nearby, a recessionary economy, changes in consumer tastes, and a price war by competitors. These are also referred to as *pure risk* (Gahin, 1967; Megginson et al., 2003).

There have been very few studies that have examined entrepreneurial risk or risk measurement; there were actually two studies. Vos (1992) examined the conceptual framework for practical risk measurement in small businesses. Ahwireng-Obeng and Mokgohlwa (2002) examined entrepreneurial risk allocation with private and public infrastructure provisions in South Africa. They categorized different risks: (a) economic risk, (b) financial risk, (c) market risk, (d) technological risk, (e) develop and construct risk, (f) start-up and operating risk, (g) socio-political risk, (h) regulatory and legal risk, and (i) *force majeure* (natural disasters) risk.

Financial risk. Financial risk is the probability of loss of money due to investment transactions. Business research has examined the utility of accounting-based measures on risk evaluation and prediction. Financial risk is often measured through *financial ratios.* There are broad categories of financial risk. *Financial failure or bankruptcy risk* is risk related to the probability of bankruptcy. *Default risk* is the risk of non-payment by a bond issuer (indicated by the firm's bond ratings). *Equity risk* is risk related to a firm's valuation and expected return. *Market risk* is the chance that a portfolio of investments can lose money due to overall swings in the financial markets.

Inflation risk is the danger that a general increase in price level will undermine the real economic value of any legal agreement that involves a fixed promise to pay over an extended period. *Interest rate risk* is market risk that stems from the fact that changing interest rates affect the value of corporate investments and obligations. *Credit risk* is the risk that another party will fail to abide by its contractual obligations. *Liquidity risk* is the difficulty of selling corporate assets or investments that have only a few willing buyers or are otherwise not easily transferable at favorable prices under typical market conditions. *Derivative risk* is the chance that volatile financial derivatives such as commodities futures and index options could create losses in underlying investments by increasing price volatility (Altma, 1968; Bodie, Kane, & Marcus, 2005; Graham & Meredith, 1937; Hickman, 1958; Hirschey, 2006; Horrigan, 1966). Further studies that examined financial risk were from more researchers (Huyghebaert & Van De Gucht, 2004; Luo, 2005; Rose, 2002; Schenk, 2002; St.-Pierre & Bahri, 2006; Volker, 2001; White, Sondhi, & Fried, 1998).

Bernstein (1990) underscored *audit risk,* the clear and present danger to lenders and investors who rely on audited financial statements. In terms of financial analysis, the analyst can identify special areas of vulnerability and the degree of audit risk present in a given situation. Assessment areas may include, but are not limited to:

- A company in difficult financial condition that urgently and frequently required credit;
- A company with high market visibility issuing frequent progress reports and earnings estimates;
- Management primarily dominated by one or a few strong willed individuals;
- Management that has displayed a propensity for earnings maximization and manipulation by various means;
- Deterioration in operating performance;
- A problem industry displaying weaknesses, in such areas as receivables inventories, cost overruns, and product dependence (p. 15).

While none of the above previously reviewed situations indicated higher audit risk individually, experience has shown that a sufficient number of these problems warranted the analyst's closer attention (Bernstein, 1990; Ireland, Kuratko, & Morris, 2006).

Financial ratios as predictors of firm performance. Much of the earlier work on financial analysis concerning risk emphasized *ratio analysis* and *financial statement examination.* Some of the authors disagree as to which key ratios are good predictors of failure Fitzpatrick (1931) conducted a 3-5-year study on trends of 13 ratios of 20 firms that failed from 1920-1929. The failed firms were compared to a control group of 19 successful firms. The conclusion of this study was that best ratio predictors were: (a) return on net worth and (b) net worth to total debt.

Winakor and Smith (1935) conducted research on a sample of 183 firms that had experienced financial difficulties for as long as 10 years prior to 1931, the year when they failed. After analyzing a10-year trend of 21 financial ratios, they concluded that *net working capital to total assets ratio* was among the most accurate and reliable indicator of failure.

Merwin (1942) conducted research on a sample of 939 firms during 1926-1936. He concluded that three key ratios were most sensitive in predicting "discontinuance" of a firm as early as four to five years before: (a) current ratio, (b) net working capital to total assets, and (c) net worth to total debt. These ratios exhibited a declining trend before the presence of discontinuance and were at all times below estimated normal ratios (Bernstein 1990). Financial ratios have proven to be reliable predictors of enterprise failure.

Many of the other early studies on the use of financial analysis and ratios for predicting failure were from Drucker (1958), Beaver (1966), and Altma (1968). Horrigan (1966) found that the bond rating changes could correctly predict to a greater extent by the use of financial ratios as opposed to random prediction of firm risk/failure. Edmister (1972) also concluded that financial ratios could predict firm failure.

Graham's "Mr. Market" allegory. One of the strongest philosophies used to explain the rudiments of market-driven speculation and behavior when selecting firms for investing was developed by Graham (2003a). In his book on investing, *"The Intelligent Investor"* Graham introduced an allegorical character, "Mr. Market" to describe the functions of the financial market in 1949. Mr. Market, lives on Wall Street, is a manic-depressive and is your hypothetical business partner; on a daily basis, he is willing to buy your interests in the business or sell you his at prevailing market prices. Mr. Market is moody, prone to manic swings from joy to despair. According to Graham's Mr. Market allegory, there are conceptual similarities that can be applied with entrepreneurial risk. For example, in terms of the market opportunity for a new venture, using the Mr. Market allegory is applicable in understanding the timing of the launch of a new venture.

Graham's "Margin-of-Safety" principle. Graham introduced another theoretical concept in 1937 called the "margin of safety" principle. This concept holds that one should not make an investment in a security unless there is a sufficient basis for believing that the price being paid is substantially lower than the value being delivered. The margin-of-safety concept is applicable to the entrepreneurial environment in this manner: the basis for starting venture should be based on return on investment (ROI). If there is not profitable return, then the margin of safety is risky. The question is whether the enterprise can leave the market before it is *unprofitable*. From a perspective of entrepreneurial risk, an entrepreneur must be familiar with Graham's margin-of-safety concept to identify opportunities for growth (Buffett, 2001; Graham, 2003b; Train, 1980).

Risk assessment. Assessing risk is a critical component in entrepreneurship. By means of exploiting opportunities, risk must be assessed as part of the process. There are complexities involved when assessing risk with opportunities.

Risk assessment factors. Entrepreneurs should screen potential ventures for their attractiveness—risks and rewards—compared to other opportunities. Several factors require consideration. Capital requirements matter to the entrepreneur who lacks access to financial markets. Entrepreneurs should favor ventures that are not capital intensive and have profit margins to sustain rapid growth with internally generated funds. Entrepreneurs should also look for a high margin for error, ventures with simple operations and low fixed costs that are less likely to face a cash crunch because of factors such as technical delays, cost overruns and slow buildup of sales (Bhide, 1999b).

Business plan and risk assessment. The connection between a business plan and risk are critical to assessing an enterprise. The investment and risk analysis is the most crucial step of the strategic business plan. Often the most omitted section of the business plan are the *benefits* and *risks* critical to the company (business enterprise); those have to be evaluated and presented to creditors and investors (Giles & Blakely, 2001). It should be noted that entrepreneurial risk could also be in the selection of the wrong business enterprise or vocation. This result is not only a significant risk, but also a failure. Why do so many businesses fail within a year or two of opening? Certainly one reason is the odds issue; most people who select a category of business to operate do not have a clue about the real probabilities of success (Stanley, 2001). Examining the risk of a venture through a business plan is critical in the determination of entrepreneurial risk.

Mainprize and Hindle (2005) performed a critical evaluation and comparison of five representative business plan evaluation aids (BPEAs). Its intent was to facilitate constructive discussion of the proposition that greater standardization of venture capital decision-making might be both desirable and possible. The five BPEAs were: (a) The Venture Opportunity Screening Guide, (b) The Bell-Mason Diagnostic, (c) The ProGrid Venture, (d) The FVRI System, and (e) The New Venture Template. They were systematically compared using a structured, taxonomic process. The findings revealed a clear superiority of BPEAs based on the researched attributes of successful ventures and the use actuarial modeling. The discussion centered on the importance of using BPEAs in a quest for greater consistency during venture capital investment decision-making.

Launch decision factors. A considerable amount of the earlier work on entrepreneurship emphasized risk behavior of the entrepreneur. The other consideration is the *risk perception* and choices entrepreneurs consider in venture selection and launch decisions. Forlani and Mullins (2000) concluded that risk perception is often a critical issue in venture launch decisions. Petrakis (2005b) also concluded that risk perception was critical in launch decision factors. However, there are advantages and disadvantages in selecting a business venture. However, it might seem most logical to choose a venture based entirely on systematic analysis of success factors. Success factors for making decisions can be of three types: (a) *head start factors,* such as technical know-how, personal contacts, physical resources, and the venture concept; (b) *the price of the venture;* and (c) *the payoff of the venture* (Vespers, 1989).

Bartlett (1999) suggested that an entrepreneur should be aware of the "risk factors" involved from a venture capitalist point of view from which the attractiveness of the opportunity is trumpeted. Bartlett (1999) identified the following factors:

- The company is in "development"—that is, most highly vulnerable—stage; its products have not been proven or marketed;
- The company's success is highly dependent on a few key individuals, none of whom have run a company of any size before;
- There are fearsome competitors on the horizon;
- The company will need more than one round of financing to survive;

- The securities are illiquid;
- Substantial "dilution" is involved;
- A few major customers form the backbone of the order bank;
- The technology is not entirely (or at all) protected by patents or copyrights. (pp. 65-66)

Phillips and Garman (2005) argued that entrepreneurship involves identification of opportunities, analysis of risk and rewards, strategic pursuit of resources and implementation of a plan of action. They concluded:

> Barriers to entrepreneurial activity include economic, organizational, and behavioral components; entrepreneurial activity also includes identifying opportunities and initiatives; and development of strategic alliances that take advantage of the benefits of entrepreneurship. (pp. 472-484)

Janney and Dess' (2006) study explored the entrepreneurial risk construct by focusing on how the decision to launch a new venture may entail risks different from those found in established firms. Opportunities often emerge from the creation of specialized knowledge: in start-ups, this knowledge is characterized by concerns for rent appropriation and information asymmetry. They concluded that traditional measures of risk do not properly account for these concerns; hence, an illusion of greater risk-taking attaches itself to entrepreneurs, especially if the specialized-knowledge is difficult to observe. They suggested alternative measures that better captured these concerns, including the dilution of control when issuing equity.

Shane (2008) provided a convincing argument that many entrepreneurs are likely to start businesses in industries that are not the best for start-up ventures; they usually start businesses in the worst industries. Rather than start businesses in industries with very few competitors, they tend to start businesses with a considerable number of competitors. The reasons behind this are:

- The industries in which people are most likely to start businesses are not the best industries for start-ups; they are often the worst;
- Rather than starting firms in industries with very few existing firms, most entrepreneurs start firms in industries where there are *a lot of firms* already in operation;
- Most entrepreneurs do not start businesses in the most financially attractive industries;
- Entrepreneurs tend to choose industries in which they are *most likely to fail*;

15

- Many entrepreneurs start businesses in industries where they have worked before and therefore understand; these industries tend to be the ones that employ the most people and are the most competitive;
- Many entrepreneurs start businesses in industries where starting a new company is easy, but businesses in industries which it is easy to get started are more failure prone than other industries;
- Many entrepreneurs start businesses in the industries in which they currently are working; that is, barbers tend to open barber-shops; chefs tend to open restaurants; and taxi drivers tend to start taxi service firms. (pp. 36-37)

Harris (1992) examined entrepreneurs' selection of ventures in bad industries. Others have further examined bad industries for start-ups (Carter, 1999; Fitzpatrick & Reynolds, 1997; Kuntze, 2001; SBA, 2007; 'Small Business at Risk,' 2007 p. 3; Taylor, 1997). Many entrepreneurs have a tendency to start *commodity-type businesses*, in which the services or products are not differentiated from each another (Buffett & Cunningham, 2005; Fridson, 2000; Goldratt, 1990; Kazem, 2003; Shane, 2008).

Success factors. Many scholarly studies of earlier date on entrepreneurial orientation and success are available to cite. The majority of the studies primarily focused on three areas: (a) common patterns of entrepreneurial success, (b) performance measures of success, and (c) entrepreneurial orientation behavior traits.

Management practices. Song (1983) examined Korean businesses in the United States. The purpose of this study was to identify common factors of management practices among successful Korean businesses in the United States and to compare them with those factors of management practices previously identified among successful American companies. Song concluded the Korean companies were:

(a) execution-oriented rather than planning-oriented; maintained simple structures of organization and small numbers of managers; (b) encouraged employees to suggest new ideas; centralized a few critical variables of management, but granted autonomy for the rest; (c) put the highest priority in human resources; (d) treated customers as major sources of information for scanning environment; (e) placed more emphasis upon personality-related factors than upon production-related factors when hiring employees; (f) directed their people with business goals and values; and expanded businesses into known areas. (pp. 140-143)

These findings also suggested that Korean companies were similar to the American companies in the following seven factors of management practice: bias for action; closeness to the customer; productivity through people; simple form, lean staff; simultaneous loose-tight properties; super-ordinate goals; and diversification with skill. Korean companies were dissimilar to American companies in autonomy and entrepreneurship.

Success constraints. Another contributing factor to entrepreneurial risk behavior in terms of success factors is human and social issues. Miaoulis, Brown, and Saunders' (2002) conducted an exploratory survey of 117 entrepreneurs (participants) in Southwestern Pennsylvania. The purpose of the study was to determine the factors they believed to be constraints on entrepreneurial success and whether these factors existed in their geographic area. The findings revealed the survey responses concerning environmental factors as constraints to start-ups: (a) state taxes are too high (78%), (b) business failure is viewed unfavorably (70%), (c) there are inconsistent policies across municipalities (68%), (d) start-up capital is too hard to get (67%), (e) the government offers insufficient incentives to start a business (66%), (f) state tax rules are too complex (64 %), and (g) the area's economic future is not bright (54%).

Failure factors. The likelihood that a new business venture will succeed (or fail) is the foundation of entrepreneurial research. It is difficult to talk about entrepreneurial risk without addressing the subject of enterprise failure. There has been a significant amount of prior research on business failure. This negative sentiment concerning failure has been expressed by many lenders of financial institutions and venture capitalists. Most new ventures do *fail*. Lenders and venture capitalists have witnessed fads, bubbles and short-term trends. Berkery (2008) argued that new companies are *guilty* until proven innocent; most of them *fail*. Investors know this. Incredibly, entrepreneurs do not or choose not to believe this; they somehow believe *their* company will different from all the others.

The later studies on failure were from Abdelsamad and Kindling (1978), and Miles, Snow and Meyer (1978). There were more recent studies from Bernstein (1990), Vos (1992), Amit, Glosten, and Muller (1993), Watson and Everett (1996), Everett and Watson (1998) and Askim (1999). The most recent studies on failure were from Bates (2005), Bee (2004), Coelho and McClure (2004), Cressy (2006), Gilmore, Carson, and O'Donnell (2004), Harting (2005), Knott and Posen (2005), Menefee and Parnell (2007), Strotmann (2007), and Michael and Combs (2008).

Other causal factors of failure. There is a recurring sentiment concerning business failure is pervasive in the prior research and literature. Abdelsamad & Kindling, (1978) essential work revealed key reasons for small-business failure:

(a) *excessive optimism*—small businessmen are often so optimistic that they fail to deal with problems promptly; (b) *inadequate board of directors*—the collection of yes-men frequently found on the board can be detrimental to the business; (c) *nepotism*—this common practice in small businesses can be detrimental to the morale of other employees; and (d) *inability to delegate*—the small businessman often neglects to train good assistants. (p. 24-32)

Peterson, Kozmetsky, and Ridgway (1983) conducted a nationwide survey of approximately 1,000 small business owners and managers. The conclusion of their study was that the major cause of small business failures is the lack of management expertise. The other findings were:

> (a) only one-third of the small business owners and managers surveyed stated that external or noncontrollable forces, such as high interest rates, federal regulations, taxes, and the economy, were the primary causes of small business failures; (b) Most cited internal or managerially controllable causes; and (c) Increased management education was the single most frequently cited suggestion for reducing small business failures. (pp. 76-95)

O'Neill & Duker (1986) conducted a study on 32 successful and 11 unsuccessful small businesses in Connecticut. The conclusions of the survey showed that:

> (a) successful firms had a lower percentage of inferior products, a lower level of debt, and a lower level of capital intensity; (b) successful firms apparently did not have a higher quality of follow-up service; (c) the only group of outside advisers that appeared to affect a firm's success was accountants; and (d) unsuccessful firms reported receiving less advice from accountants. (pp. 15-35)

In another study, Amit, Glosten, & Muller (1993) study examined why some new ventures succeeded while others failed. They theorized that there are some fundamental unanswered questions on failure, for which there does not exist a cohesive explanatory, predictive, or normative theory. In this article, they identify major challenges for entrepreneurship theory development, and offer insights into promising directions for future research. They concluded that it might be too ambitious to expect a complete and robust theory due to the interdisciplinary nature of entrepreneurship. Furthermore, they showed that by integrating perspectives and by applying analytic, empirical and experimental tools from a range of fields, some of the fundamental questions on failure or success could be answered.

Watson and Everett's (1996) study sought to clarify a number of apparent misconceptions concerning small business failure, in the hope that prospective entrepreneurs may be more reliably informed about the risks involved. The results may also help to ensure that future policy decisions made by governments, financial institutions, and other groups with an interest in small business are more soundly based. They collected data on failure rates on 5,196 small business start-ups. Data was collected in 51 managed shopping centers across the five mainland states of Australia and covering the period 1961-1990. The reported failure rates varied from a high of more than 9% per annum to a low of less than 1% per annum depending on the choice of failure definition.

In a subsequent study, Everett and Watson (1998) explored the impact of macro-economic factors on small business mortality. There were the categories of small business risk factors; causes of business failure; and definitions of small business failure. Model of the relationship between small business failure rates and risk factors. In a later study, Everett and Watson (1999) study concluded that *economic factors* appear to be a factor in 30 to 50% of small business failures (e.g. lagging employment rates, interest rates and others). Osborne (1993) asserted the reasons for entrepreneurial failure:

(a) *undercapitalization,* many entrepreneurs grossly underestimate their need for capital; (b) *poor planning,* many entrepreneurs fail to design and deliver to meet the needs of the customer. Some locate their businesses poorly and fail to properly conduct market research; (c) *lack of expertise and credibility,* many entrepreneurs get involved with businesses that are beyond their sphere of expertise; and (d) *poor money management,* many businesses fail because their managers get into a cash flow bind; (e) *failure to follow regulations with government entities;* and (f) *lack of managerial skill,* many entrepreneurs are great at creating dazzling plans but fail in the implementation and the management of people. (p. 18)

To operationalize the term "failure", Watson and Everett (1996) cited five definitions to describe that have been used (or suggested) to describe enterprise failure:

(1) *discontinuance,* all businesses that are sold or cease to operate are classified as having failed (discontinuance of ownership); (2) *bankruptcy,* only businesses that enter into bankruptcy are considered to have failed; (3) *termination* to prevent further losses; (4) *inability,* an inability to "make a go of it," and (5) the notion that only businesses that cease to exist should be regarded as failures (discontinuance of business). (pp. 45-62)

Furthermore, Watson and Everett reported the average annual failure rates varied considerably from a high of more than 9% when failure was defined as *discontinuance of ownership*, to a low of less than 1% when bankruptcy was the measure of failure used. Between these extremes, failure rates of about 4% are reported when failure was defined as either *failed to "make a go of it"* or *discontinuance of business*, and a failure rate of about 2% is reported using the definition disposed of to prevent further losses. The cumulative failure rate at the end of ten years ranged from a high of 64.2 % using discontinuance of ownership as the definition of failure, to a low of 5.3% using bankruptcy as the definition of failure (Watson & Everett, 1996).

Yrle, Hartman, and Yrle-Fryou (2000) identified two key reasons to explain small business failure. First is *poor management*. At least 90 percent of business failures were due to internal sources such as incompetence, neglect, and a lack of experience; thus, poor preparation leads to failure. Second, is a *poor economy*. There was a heavy rate of small business failures accompanying the era of the Great Depression. The widespread belief is that an increase in business failures is indicative of a weakness in the economy (Yrle, Hartman & Yrle-Fryou, 2000).

Gilmore, Carson, and O'Donnell (2004) theorized that there is a strong association between small business owner-managers/entrepreneurs and risk by virtue of the high failure rates of small firms. The objective of this study was to uncover situations encountered by owner-managers/entrepreneurs that they perceived to involve an element of risk. It sought to understand how owner-managers behave when faced with such "risky" situations. A qualitative study was undertaken with owner-managers of small firms operating in a wide spectrum of industry settings. While a great variation was encountered between the entrepreneurs, areas of commonality were distilled and it was shown that the key situations owner-managers deemed to be risky were those pertaining to cash flow, company size, entering new markets or new areas of business, and entrusting staff with responsibilities. Furthermore, it was shown that the two key tools used to manage these risky situations where the use of managerial competencies and networking (Gilmore, Carson & O'Donnell 2004; Leyden & Link 2004).

Santarelli and Vivarelli (2007) study highlighted three key themes that they felt were areas of concern with firm formation and survival and the growth of new-born firms. Their study's basic purpose was to single out the microeconomic entrepreneurial foundations of industrial dynamics (entry and exit) and to characterize the founder's ex - ante features in terms of likely expost business performance. They concluded that the entry of new firms was heterogeneous with innovative entrepreneurs being found together with: (a) passive followers; (b) over-optimist gamblers; and (c) even escapees from unemployment. Since the founders were heterogeneous and may have made "entry mistakes," policy incentives should be highly selective, favoring nascent entrepreneurs endowed with progressive motivation and promising predictors of better business performance.

Enterprise failure in industry types. Some studies have taken a different approach by looking at certain types of industry failure types. Ricketts, Gaskill, Van Auken, and Manning (1993) examined failed (discontinued) small businesses. They focused on SMEs in the apparel and accessory retailing industry between 1987 and 1991. They found that perceived failure factors of discontinued small business apparel and accessory retailers clustered in four factors:

1. Factor 1 – inadequate knowledge of pricing strategies, failure to generate a long-term business plan, ineffective advertising/promotional strategy, lack of managerial experience, skills, and training; failure to generate a personnel plan; lack of experience in the product line, inflexible decision-making, lack of knowledge of current business literature, poor use of outside advisors, and ineffective interior store layout patter;
2. Factor 2 – poor relations, difficulties in receiving merchandise, inadequate financial accounting or record keeping;
3. Factor 3 – competition from discount retailers, inability to compete in trade area, failure to offer saleable merchandise assortments; and
4. Factor 4 – premature business growth/overextension, inventory difficulties (pp. 24-26).

Following a similar research approach to Ricketts et al. (1993), Gaskill, Van Auken and Manning (1993) conducted a study on the perceived causes of small business failure. Their study examined perceived causes of small business failure in the apparel and accessory retailing industry. Their study found that perceived failure factors of discontinued small business apparel and accessory retailers clustered in four area: (1) poor managerial functions, (2) capital management, (3) competitive environment, and (5) growth and expansion. The external business environment is an area perceived to contribute to business failure. Items such as "poor relations with vendors," "difficulties in receiving merchandise," "competition from discount stores," "inability to compete in trading area" and "failure to offer saleable merchandise assortments" suggested that failed small business owners were ineffective in functioning in the environment in which they operated. They concluded that while the study results showed that apparel and accessory small business failures were a result of poor performance and inefficiencies in four general areas, neither the factors nor the variables within each factor should be viewed as being independent. The small business firm operates in a dynamic environment where the effects of poor managerial performance and changing environmental characteristics permeate throughout the organization.

In a follow-up study to their 1998 study, Everett and Watson (1998) concluded that *economic factors* appear to be a factor in 30 to 50% of small business failures (e.g. lagging employment rates, interest rates, and others).

Parsa, Self, Njite, & King (2005) study explored restaurant ownership turnover rates using qualitative data, longitudinal data (1996-1999), and data from Dunn and Bradstreet reports. Results of their study indicated marginal differences in restaurant failures between franchise chains (57.2 %) and independent operators (61.4 %). Restaurant density and ownership turnover were strongly correlated ($r = .9919$). A qualitative analysis indicated that effective management of family life cycle and quality-of-life issues is more important than previously believed in the growth and development of a restaurant. (pp. 304-322)

Some businesses are more financially vulnerable to failure based on the business design and industry. For example, farmers are most vulnerable. Gutter and Saleem (2005) concluded that financial vulnerability was determined by the extent to which income and wealth are derived from the same source. Their findings suggested that business owners face unique financial vulnerability because of their reliance on the business as both a source of income and wealth. Business owners may have insufficient diversification when relying on the business as an asset to fund retirement. Among business owners, farmers are the most vulnerable; their proportions of total income and total portfolio attributable to the business are higher than other business types.

In a study of failure concerning firms in high technological environments, Menefee & Parnell (2007) made three notable observations:

> (a) a competent and technologically current company staff was found to be the most important factor for high-tech firms, but only somewhat important for low-tech firms. In addition, human resource management issues were more important for high-tech firms than for their low-tech counterparts. Thus, these findings highlight the importance of quality people matter in technology businesses; (b) the development of new products and services was much less important for low-tech firms than for high-tech firms. In other words, low-tech businesses do not necessarily need to be concerned with new products or services as long as the delivery of existing products and services are implemented effectively; and (c) lastly they concluded it is possible, if not likely that success and failure factors will vary across industries. (pp. 60-73)

Strotmann (2007) conducted an empirical analysis on the determinants of new-firm survival in the manufacturing sector of Baden-Wuerttemberg (Germany) from 1981 to 1994. The analysis focused on firm- and industry-specific determinants of new-firm survival. A possible effect of regional agglomeration and of the business cycle was also tested, albeit in a very general manner. From a methodical point of view parametric and semiparametric duration models are used. Grouped duration models are estimated taking into account the problem of ties. Moreover, the problem of unobserved heterogeneity was considered, which was so far been neglected in numerous studies. The empirical analyses show with respect to industry-specific effects that the risk of new-firm failure is the larger the larger an industry' s minimum efficient scale is, the worse the sectoral demand-conditions are, the more narrow the market is, the higher dynamics of foundation within an industry are. The liability of smallness-hypothesis is confirmed for German manufacturing while with respect to firm age the results favor the liability of adolescence-hypothesis instead of a pure liability of newness.

Failure due to industry decline. Entrepreneurial risk is very apparent with industries that are in a state of decline in the product life cycle. Enterprise failure is also attributed to *industry decline.* Porter (1989) illustrated the major characteristics of declining industries: (a) *technological substitution,* this can be threatening to industry profits because increasing substitution usually depresses profits at the same time it cuts into sales; (b) *demographics,* this is shrinkage in the size of the customer group that purchases the product, thus the demographics cause the decline by reducing demand in downstream industries; and (c) *shifts in needs,* demand can fall because of sociological or other reasons which change buyers' needs or tastes (Porter, 1989).

Effects of failure. Much of the earlier work emphasized financial causes of enterprise failure; much of the earlier work examined the complexities of enterprise failure. However, some studies have taken a different approach with a new inquiry. Coelho and McClure's (2004) study explored the benefits of failures, and uses aspects of the analogy between death and business failure to analyze how failures in business economize upon resources and lead to better firms and greater efficiencies. Risk-taking in the absence of knowledge and a realistic assessment of the probabilities is simply *gambling.* The data revealed that a number of individuals have been unsuccessful in overcoming certain barriers.

Harting (2005) concluded that although some family households undoubtedly do lose money when a business fails, most escape relatively unscathed by exiting quickly rather than persisting in the face of an unfavorable business environment. This behavior has implications for how we interpret liquidity constraints to entrepreneurship, as well as for government policy in support of small businesses. The findings of this study suggested that entrepreneurs face many and unique *external forces* that have been highly influential on enterprise failure.

Knott and Posen (2005) theorized that the conventional wisdom thinks of failure as wasteful. They concluded that approximately 80-90 % of new firms ultimately fail. However, they examined whether there are economic benefits to offset business failure as wasteful. They characterized three potential mechanisms through which excess entry affects market structure, firm behavior, and efficiency, and then test them in the banking industry. The results indicated that failed firms generate *externalities* that significantly and substantially reduce industry cost. On average, these benefits exceed the private costs of the entrants. They concluded that failure appeared to be good for the economy.

Enterprise behavior characteristics and orientation. There has been significant research on enterprise characteristics in terms of firm behavior and orientation. Not all small-to-medium business enterprises (SMEs) engage in exploiting new markets; thus they are not considered "entrepreneurial" based on their behavior (Drucker, 1985). Tandon's (1987) research examined the investment in start-up ventures and the ventures' risk levels. Because a reduced failure rate is desirable for investors, the economy, and society, this research sought to build a theory by developing a robust, and comprehensive framework of new venture performance. Traditional academic disciplines, economics, psychology, management, and new literature on entrepreneurship were reviewed and augmented with practitioner prescriptions. The resulting model had 101 factors in "four dimensions of risk: (i) individual, (ii) opportunity, (iii) resources, and (iv) "venture plans" (pp. 235-248).

Tandon developed a measurement and scoring method for each of the 101 factors meeting the objective of developing a multidimensional scale measuring a higher score with higher performance. Tandon's research classified 25 new ventures based in Minneapolis/St. Paul according to this scale. Performance was ranked according to financial criteria relevant for investors and grouped as "Successful" and "Unsuccessful." Information was collected from pre-start-up business plans, circulars were offered [*sic*], annual reports, and other documents. This data was augmented with an in-depth structured interview of the entrepreneurs.

The results of Tandon's study indicated there were statistically significant differences between the scores of the two groups. Tandon concluded the dimensions of opportunity and venture plans were significantly related to venture performance; whereas the dimensions of individual characteristics and resources were not significant. Since each venture had undergone prior investor scrutiny, the scale could only be applied in the future to ventures that had survived a similar initial scrutiny. The lack of significance denotes either a perfect extraction of information by investors or, more likely, a lack of sharpness of the measuring methods.

There have been noteworthy studies on Entrepreneurial Orientation (EO). Lumpkin (1996) examined the entrepreneurial orientation (EO) of firms is a central concept in the study of strategic management from an earlier study by Miles and Snow (1978). The EO Model consisted of innovativeness, risk taking, proactiveness, and competitive aggressiveness. Prior theory and research suggested that an entrepreneurial orientation is a key ingredient for organizational success. The conclusions of the study suggested that elements of an EO were vital to the success of young firms. However, for new entrants, the relationship of the four dimensions with environment and structure may not have been useful in predicting the level of success; and the dimensions of EO did not constitute a unidimensional strategic orientation. The findings indicated that the moderating influence of environment and structure on the EO-performance relationship was rather weak. The innovativeness and proactiveness dimensions exhibited positive main effects; correlational analysis indicated that the four dimensions of EO did vary independently to a greater extent than they conveyed.

Aloulou and Fayolle (2005) concluded that: (a) an innovative small business was not entrepreneurial if it did not take risks, or was not sufficiently proactive towards competitors and environment; (b) EO's importance as a valid strategic orientation for small businesses was apparent when they rethought their strategic analyses with opportunity-based and resource-based views; and (c) adoption of such orientation seemed to reflect a needed conciliation between other strategic orientations (market-based, technology-based and stakeholder-based orientations) and the blending of them.

Family-owned enterprises. There have been some family-related studies on entrepreneurship; they have taken a different approach in a typical study of this type. Hollman and Mohammad-Zadeh (1984) examined risk taking in family firms. Zahra (2006) further highlighted the issues of family firm's conservatism and unwillingness to take risk associated with entrepreneurial activities. Over time, some family firms become conservative and unwilling to take the risks associated with entrepreneurial activities. As a result, he adopted a broad definition of entrepreneurial risk taking. His study used *agency theory* to highlight key correlates of risk taking among 209 family-owned U.S. manufacturing firms. He concluded that family ownership and involvement promoted entrepreneurship, whereas the long tenures of CEO founders tended to have the opposite effect. These results urged managers to capitalize on the skills and talents of their family members in promoting entrepreneurship and selective venturing into new market arenas. Furthermore, the founder and family-related variables clearly exerted an important influence on risk taking in ways that have not been captured in the literature.

Theoretical Basis for Instrument Development

The dimensions of entrepreneurial risk used for this study were developed from many texts and scholarly research articles on entrepreneurship, small business, and risk. As stated previously, there are few studies that have focused exclusively on enterprise risk. The underlying concepts concerning entrepreneurial risk (ER) used for this study are illustrated in the following five categories: (a) personal characteristics, (b) intangible operation risks, (c) enterprise operation risks, (d) market climate risks, and (e) business environment risks.

Personal characteristics risk forces. This dimension of entrepreneurial risk classification reflects the individual attributes of the entrepreneur in

25

terms of risk level. Shane (2008) identifies five demographic traits in the personal characteristics dimension of the ER factors. These traits are interrelated but conceptually and theoretically distinct categories: (a) *gender*, males are twice as likely as females to be involved in starting a new business at any point in time and females have higher failure rates; (b) *age*, the highest rate of self-employed people and business ownership is between the ages of 45 and 64 with the most common range for founders between the ages of 35 and 44; (c) *education level*, the more education one attains the more likely an individual will start their own business; (d) *education field type*, business majors are more likely than other majors to start their own business; (e) *ethnicity*, the ethnicity of the individual plays a significant role in the failure or success of a business enterprise. Blacks are 50% less likely than Whites to get a new business up and running within seven years of beginning the start-up process. Blacks also exit from self-employment at twice the rate of their White counterparts.

Industry experience. Industry experience is a significant consideration in minimizing risk with the small-to-medium business enterprise. Lack of industry experience can influence failure or success in a business enterprise. Why do so many businesses fail within a year or two of opening? Most people who select a category of business to operate are not aware of the real probabilities of success (Barrese, 2003; McCormack, 1984; Parhankangas & Hellström, 2007; Shane, 2008; Stanley & Danko, 1996; Trump & Schwartz, 1987; Vespers, 1989).

There are both advantages and disadvantages in selecting a business venture. Lenders, buyers, and sellers will pay attention to the stability and management skills of the business owner (Busenitz, 1999; McCormack, 1984; Stanley, 2001; Sutton, 2003; Trump & Schwartz, 1987). Sam Walton, founder of the global giant Wal-Mart, discovered his expertise in retailing early in his career and built a multi-million dollar corporation (Slater, 2003; Trimble, 1990; Walton & Huey, 1992).

Parhankangas and Hellström's (2007) study was based on a survey sent to 142 Swedish and Finnish venture capitalists, with a response rate of 63% (90 responses). The results of their research showed that:

> (a) *experience* drives the perception of risk and the riskiness of the preferred investment portfolio. More specifically this attributed to the presence of more pronounced perceptions of market and agency risk, partly stemming from their experience, investors seemed to be willing to take more risks; this result may be attributed to overconfidence, illusion of control, or the speculative dimension of risk present in entrepreneurial settings; (b) the portfolio risk is dynamically attenuated by the execution of various risk reduction strategies, such as syndication, information seeking, monitoring and the use of preferred stock and (c) venture capitalists are proactive and respon-

sible risk takers, who shield themselves from potential losses through a careful application of risk reduction strategies, but also that their responses to risk may resemble more the behavior of typical entrepreneurs than that of typical managers. (pp. 183-205)

Gerber (1995) discussed the concept of "Fatal Assumption," which theorized that if a person understands the technical side of a business, they would understand a business that does technical work. Personality characteristics influence the "fatal assumption" theory. The fatal assumption that influences entrepreneurial risk is the assumption that if a person has prior experience in an industry, they could *successfully operate a business enterprise in that industry*. This is the essence of the "fatal assumption" in terms of entrepreneurship (e.g. "The Peter Principle").

Education. Stanley (2001) argued that it is not how much you study and how long, it is *what you study* and how well it can be *leveraged* in the business world. Pick a long shot and your college degree may not be enough to save you; pick a winner and the law of economics may not punish you for never spending a day in college. One must be highly motivated and selective to succeed in a particular vocation. New entrepreneurs must learn how to *specialize* and *monopolize* (Shane, 2008; Stanley, 2001).

Gender. According to some of the prior studies on gender and entrepreneurship, there are differences in terms of entrepreneurial behavior and business ownership characteristics. In a study on gender differences between men and women-owned businesses, Collins (2007) examined gender differences and their relationship to entrepreneurial behavior in terms of Entrepreneurial Quotient (EQ) personality traits. Collins used 11 EQ scales to examine differences along gender lines. His conclusions were that there were significant differences between men and women entrepreneurs concerning personality traits: (a) *education* did not impact entrepreneurial success in terms of gender; (b) there were differences in EQ scales by gender; (c) *males* tended to score higher on measures of adaptability, risk tolerance, time management and extroversion; (d) *females* scored higher on measures of planning, goal orientation, intuition, and perception; and (e) *males and females* significantly differed in terms of personal satisfaction, financial rewards, recognition, and building relationships with customers. Other researchers reached similar findings on gender differences and its relationship to entrepreneur behavioral (e.g., Browne, 2001; Kazem, 2003; Robb, 2002; Shane, 2008).

The prior research seems to be consistent in the conclusions that female-owned businesses generally underperformed male-owned businesses on a variety of measures. These measures include revenue, profit, growth, and discontinuance (failure) rates. Watson (2003) conducted a study on a representative sample of 8,375 small and medium-sized Australian enterprises that originally were surveyed in 1994-95. He also did a follow-up survey in each of the subsequent three years for a subsample of businesses. The aim here was to determine whether female-owned businesses exhibit higher failure rates than male-owned businesses and to determine, whether this finding persists, after controlling for industry differences. He concluded from the results that, while female-owned businesses do have higher failure rates when compared to male-owned businesses, the difference is not significant after controlling for the effects of industry (Watson, 2003).

Ethnicity. Prior scholarly literature has examined the personal risk behavior of entrepreneurs. Some of the prior literature on business survival rates has concluded that those survival rates were attributed to gender and racial factors. Robb (2002) compared survival rate variances between men and women-owned business start-ups and also between minority-and non-minority-owned business start-ups. Robb concluded that survival rates of businesses were attributed to gender, racial factors, and some non-racial factors. The conclusions of the study were: (a) Asian-owned businesses actually fared better than non-minority-owned businesses; (b) however, Black-owned and Hispanic-owned businesses fared worse than White-owned businesses; (c) in terms of gender and racial differences, Black-owned businesses and women-owned fared better than Black-owned businesses that were owned by men (p. 396).

Ethnicity and gender. In addition, concerning the variable of race, when *ethnicity* and *gender* were considered together, the differences were perhaps even more striking: businesses owned by Asian females had the highest survival rate at 52.5%, followed closely by Asian males with 52.2%; White males and females followed at 49.3% and 47.3% respectively; Hispanic males had a survival rate of 45.4% as compared with 39.8% for Hispanic females; and Black- and women-owned businesses fared better than Black-owned businesses that were owned by men; businesses owned by Black males had the lowest survival rate at 33.8% while Black females fared somewhat better than Black males with a survival rate of 36.9%. The conclusions from this study indicated that women-owned businesses were still less likely to survive than men-owned businesses. The study also indicated that Black and Hispanic-owned businesses were less likely to survive than businesses owned by Whites, while Asian-owned businesses were more likely to survive (Robb, 2002). Shane (2008) reached similar conclusions from his study on entrepreneurship success and ethnicity.

Wages/compensation from the enterprise. Several studies have compared what entrepreneurs earn compared to their non-entrepreneur counterparts. Some scholarly literature has examined the income or wages from the entrepreneurs compensate themselves from the enterprise. This risk variable involved examines if the SME's profitability provides a return on investment (ROI) in terms of compensation to the entrepreneur. Shane (2008) revealed some interesting facts concerning what entrepreneurs actually earn from their enterprises. His conclusions were:

On average self-employed persons earned significantly less than the average person who worked for someone; the median earnings of people who have operated their own business for 10 years earned 35% lower than what they would have earned working for someone else; those who had operated their own business up to 25 years, the gap shrinked to 25%; no matter how long the entrepreneur has owned the business, they still earned less than the entry-level salary for someone performing the same occupation but employed by someone else; and entrepreneurs had more variable income compared to their non-entrepreneur counterparts, which could lead to the risk of downward mobility. (p. 101)

Intangible operations risks forces. The intangible operation dimension reflects the intangible risks that are an implicit influence to the operation of the enterprise. Intangible operation risks play an important part in the dynamics of the enterprise. Intangible operations consist of three interrelated vectors: business entity type, capital investment intensity, and time intensity dependence.

Business entity type. A good entity is one that shields and protects the business owner's personal assets from business risk. Sole proprietorships and general partnerships provide no asset protection. Sole proprietorships and partnerships are the most risky entities and should be avoided (Kiyosaki & Lechter 2001; Sutton, 2001). Good entities such as a Limited Liability Corporation (LLC), Limited Liability Partnership (LLP), or a corporation (Chapter S or Chapter C) limit the liability of risk takers (Kennedy, 2001; Lechter, 2001; Miles, 2006; Sutton, 2001; Taliento, 2007). Golis (2002) advocates that entrepreneurs should adopt public company structures (LLC, LLP, or corporation) as preparation for a possible public listing. The current taxation environment firmly supports setting up such a company (Golis, 2002).

Capital investment intensity. This risk measures capital intensity as a vital consideration in starting a business enterprise. The more capital needed for the venture, the bigger the financial risk. Most entrepreneurs start their businesses for less than $25,500 (Shane, 2008). The investment and risk analysis is the most crucial step of the strategic business plan (Bartlett, 1999; Berkery, 2008; Fiet & Patel, 2006; Formani, 2001; Giles & Blakely, 2001; Kennedy, 2001; Khavul, 2001; Lechter, 2001; Miles, 2006; Psaltopoulos, Stathopoulou, & Skuras, 2005; Sutton, 2001).

Owner time dependency. There is a difference in ownership types. *Active ownership* is the active involvement, ownership and participation in the day-to-day operations. *Passive ownership* is the financial investment in the business only, without involvement in the day-to-day operations (Cantillon, trans. 2003; Ferriss, 2007; Kiyosaki & Lechter, 2001). This risk focuses on the firm's dependency on the entrepreneur's presence in the business and its effect on profitability. A business is risky if the profitability of the business is solely dependent on the owner's presence in the firm.

Other intangible forces and influences. There are several other intangible forces that affect the SME's profitability. *Patent infringement* considers the potential risk of legal action. *Fixed assets* "considers the requirements for the business that are product specific and banks may be hesitant to loan against because of their low resale value." (Dollinger, 1999; p. 45). *Fluctuations in the business cycle* considers the economic fluctuations such as recessions and depressions that may be an influence. *Risk concerning unstable interest rates and inflation rates* considers the changes in the economic climate that may be an influence. *Significant delays in receiving payments from customers* considers the threats for the survival of the firm in the first year given its projected cash needs in the first six months (Dollinger, 1999; Johnson 1998; Winfrey & Budd, 1999). The distinction of the intangible operation dimension is that it is frequently exhibited in SME firms by means of implicit influences.

Enterprise operation risk forces. The enterprise operation dimension reflects the operational aspects and characteristics that are explicit risks to operation of the enterprise. The enterprise operation dimension plays an important part in the dynamics of the enterprise. The enterprise operation dimension is comprised of seven interrelated vectors.

Labor/operating costs. These are the risks involved with labor costs in the enterprise operation. Labor costs can demand a capital-intensive process incorporating automated, high-semiannual output machinery or a labor-intensive process that employs many people and general-purpose equipment with low productivity capacity (Ball, McClulloch, Frantz, Geringer, & Minor, 2006; Bygrave, 1994; Miles, 2006; Shane, 2008).

Equipment systems investment. These are the risks involved with the investment in specialized equipment; for example, oil exploration is much more speculative than a pizza restaurant. Potential profits in the oil exploration industry are huge, and so are the losses (Joseph, Nekoranec, & Steffens, 1993; Miles, 2006; Psaltopoulos, Stathopoulou, & Skuras, 2005).

Diseconomies of scale/Internet. This is the risk that is differentiated from the industrial-based "economies of scale", because the company has the ability to substitute *cheap information* for human labor as a resource (Hirschey & Pappas, 1992; McInerney & White, 2000; Miles, 2006; Turner, 2003). From an economic perspective, diseconomies of scale (DOS) also occurs when the long run average cost per unit rises with an increase in output; it is also the long term average cost of production as the scale of operations increases past a projected targeted point (Hirschey, 2006, p. 133). DOS is the opposite of economies of scale. For the purposes of this study, DOS is applied in terms of risk that is based on the ability of the SME to minimize constraints in the supply chain (McInerney & White, 2000). They pose entrepreneurial risk for SMEs that cannot exploit supply chain advantages. An SME can minimize entrepreneurial risk through use of a competitive advantage with *disintermediaries.*

One of the key reasons many SMEs in the retail industry fail against Wal-Mart is because they lack a competitive advantage in the DOS and supply chain management. The supply chain process is as follows: (a) raw materials, (b) transportation, (c) manufacturing, (d) distribution, and (e) retail showroom. The components of the supply chain process have distinct participants. First are the *producers.* These are two types of organizations: the producers of the *raw materials*; then manufacturer, the producers of the *finished products.* Second are the *distributors,* (also known as *wholesalers*). These are the companies that take inventory in bulk from the producers and deliver a bundle of related product lines to customers. They typically sell products to businesses in large quantities, typically do not sell to individual consumers. Third are the *retailers.* They are the companies that stock inventory and sell in smaller quantities to the *end customer or general public* in retail stores. Last, are the *customers*, which are the end-users, individuals or organizations that purchases and uses the product in order to consume it (Hugos, 2003). These are the many *intermediaries* in the supply chain process.

The firm that can reach the customer with the fewest intermediaries in the supply chain process *wins.* This competitive advantage of *disintermediaries* streamlines the process of getting the product to the end-user. This competitive advantage of disintermediaries streamlines the process of getting the product to the end-user. By expediently bypassing the traditional supply chain process: (a) raw materials to the manufacturer; (b) then from the manufacturer to the wholesaler; and (c) then retailer to the consumer. Considering some SMEs strategically bypass the quintessential supply chain process, many of the SMEs cannot compete in the traditional supply chain process.

An excellent case of a firm that circumvents the traditional supply chain process, because of their strategic implementation of DOS is Dell Computers. By exploiting their competitive advantage of DOS, Dell Computers eliminated three of the four components in the supply chain and created a new model: from the manufacturer direct to the consumer (also known as, "Direct from Dell") (Dell & Fredman, 1999). This enabled Dell to pass those savings on to their customers and made their computers price competitive against their retail competitors in the marketplace.

Internet/disintermediation. The concept of disintermediation is an example of the powerful influence of the internet. The internet has a tendency to *disintermediate* and destroy traditional businesses and industries. This is the case of online business models (e-commerce) *displacing* physical businesses (brick and mortar). The disintermediating power of the Internet can attack any industry and market sector, most particularly established businesses. The Internet has created powerful diseconomies of scale (McInerney & White, 2000, p. 72). The Internet disintermediates everything it touches, causing casualties. Traditional businesses built on economies of scale now have to compete on *econo-*

mies of scope. In addition to the threat of disintermediation, traditional book retailers in one country now must compete for customers in other countries. The point of the sale is now the *computer* and geography is *meaningless* (Knopper, 2009; McInerney & White, 2000; Sandino, 2004).

A perfect example of the disintermediation concept is the emergence of on-line book retailer Amazon.com. Amazon had revenues of $600 million in its first year (1999). Amazon grabbed 80% of the on-line book market. As Amazon's market share increased, independent bookstores' market share decreased (McInerney & White, 2000). Amazon's growth and success caused the collapse of the independent retail bookstore. Amazon *disintermediated* the retail bookstore market and *displaced* retail bookstores. The cost structure of brick-and mortar retailers has been completely undermined (Knopper, 2009; McInerney & White, 2000).

Business design risk. A risk to traditional SME firms is the inability to convert the conventional business design to a digital business design. *Digital business design* is the conversion of a conventional business to e-commerce platform; this enables those firms to compete electronically. Many firms deceive themselves into thinking that they can move into this new model incrementally. A digital business design can work within the framework of a traditional business structure. However, this conversion takes *years* (Slywotzky, Morrison, Andelman, Moser, Mundt, & Quella, 1999). For example, Amazon, Dell Computers, Ebay, and Charles Schwab were all successful in converting from a traditional business design to a *digital business design.* For example, Amazon forced Barnes and Noble, Borders, and other traditional book retailers to convert to a digital business design just to compete with them.

Protection mechanisms. These risks are concerned with the processes by which a business protects itself against a crisis within the business firm with a team of advisors. For example, a tax attorney would provide tax advice to take advantage of tax-loopholes; Another example is the relationship with a banker for venture capital for an acquisition (Gerber, 1995; Kennedy, 2001; Sutton, 2003).

Intellectual property risk. This is the protection risk concerning the firm's intellectual property, such as trademarks, patents, copyrights, and trade secrets. This risk is critical for a firm to protect their intellectual capital. A business enterprise can be at serious risk in regards to intellectual property (Lechter, 2003; Sutton, 2001; Sutton, 2003).

Velocity of profit. This is the risk concerning the speed of profitability within the business enterprise. This concept was introduced by the late Dave Thomas, of Wendy's Restaurant, International. The speed of the profitability is how promptly the enterprise is paid for its goods and services (Miles, 2003; Thomas, 1991).

Customer turnover/turnaround. This is the rate of activity at which the enterprise moves customers through the business. This risk variable is based on the concept of inventory turnover in accounting. This risk variable determines how rapidly a business turns over customers in the business enterprise (Ayres, 2007; Farris, Bendle, Pfeifer, & Reibstein, 2006; Koch, 2003; Miles, 2006; Spector, 2003; Taylor & Smalling-Archer, 1994). Business activity or customer activity can be at risk in terms of customer activity. A firm's profitability is driven by customer activity. In order to manage customer relationships, a firm must be able to count its customers, in terms of risk and customer management. A firm can use three primary metrics to accomplish this: (a) *customer counts*, the number of customers of a firm for a specific time period; (b) *recency*, this is the length of time since a customer's last purchase, for example, a six-month customer is one who has purchased items from the firm at least once within the last six months; and (c) *retention rate*, which is the ratio of the number of retained customers that make a repeat purchase in the same business (Farris, Bendle, Pfeifer, & Reibstein, 2006 p. 101)

From another perspective, businesses should not think of products or services on one hand and time on the other. One should think of *product-time* and *service-time* as one. For example, if a firm could provide a much faster way for getting an existing product or service to the customers, it could change its economics and offer a terrific new business opportunity. The risk here is the when an enterprise ignores product-time and service-time (Koch, 2003).

Market climate risk forces. Market forces can affect the success or failure of SMEs. Invariably, an enterprise is at risk when there are a significantly high number of similar products in the market place. As there are good and bad industries for SMEs, there are industries with a high market saturation of products and services.

Market potential. This examines the potential risk of a new product/service to carve out a niche in the market. New businesses owners must: (a) position themselves in markets where the competition is low or nonexistent, or not dominant (Dollinger, 2002; Gordon, 2007; Hirschey, 2006); (b) target markets that are too small for the giants (Taylor & Small-Archer, 1994; Longenecker, Moore & Palich, 2006); (c) target markets that value service above price; (d) target areas where the competition does not do well or products/services that the competition does not sell; and (e) find a need and fill it (Lowenstein, 1995; Psaltopoulos, Stathopoulou, & Skuras, 2005; Schumpter 1975; Tybout, & Sternthal, 2001; White, Sondhi, & Fried, 1998).

Market entry/exit barriers. This measures the risk of market entry and exit within the business enterprise. There is high risk involved with the business enterprise trying to enter and exit a market sector. Researchers agree that start-up enterprises have certain risk characteristics but they do not agree on why. Entry barriers include government regulation, the need for capital investment in equipment and market dominance from the incumbents (Fridson, 2000; Porter, 1985; Porter, 1989; Santarelli & Vivarelli, 2007; Shane, 2005). New entrants (nascent) firms may find themselves at a disadvantage relative to incumbents due to the existence of entry barriers. There are four primary types of forces that have historically been barriers-to-entry: precommittment contracts; licenses and patents; experience-curve effects; and a pioneering-brand advantage (Oster, 1990; Shane, 2005).

From a marketing perspective, Forlani and Mullins (2001) study focused on new venture market entry risk. They theorized that among the most critical elements in the development of any new venture are the entrepreneur's analyses and decisions regarding entry into new and sometimes uncharted markets. Their conclusions were that: (a) early entry was judged as more appropriate for markets where the likelihood of loss or gain is relatively more uncertain, compared to more certain markets. In the latter kinds of markets, follower strategies maybe more appropriate; (b) for markets in which the magnitude of the required investment was substantial, where the magnitude of possible losses and gains is high, a broader entry, rather than a niche strategy, is called for; and (c) both risk propensity and risk perceptions influence both the timing and the scale of market entry that successful entrepreneurs will prefer. (pp. 136-137)

Huyghebaert and Van De Gucht (2004) examined the forces that shape the post-entry exit probability of entrepreneurial start-ups, with an emphasis on the impact of incumbents' strategic behavior in financial markets. They found that entrepreneurial start-ups in highly competitive industries were more likely to exit and that leverage compounds this exit risk. However, the latter result only held when potential adverse selection and moral hazard problems in financial markets are large at start-up. Under these circumstances, competitors could negatively influence creditors' perceptions on entrepreneurial quality or behavior through aggressive strategic actions to impede future financing and induce the start-up's exit.

Hatala (2005) examined six key barriers that were areas of concern for the individuals' decision to start a business. Those examined forces that negatively affect an individual's decision to start a business were vital to the thought process. Factor analysis yielded a six-barrier construct: lack of confidence, personal problems, lack of skills, start-up logistics, financial needs; and time constraints. The instrument was also administered to a test group of new entrepreneurs participating in a training program to determine pre- and post-test intervention effects.

In a subsequent study, Huyghebaert and Van de Gucht (2007) hypothesized that start-up enterprises in growing industries had a lower leverage but raised more bank debt. Their study focused on business start-ups and concluded such ventures lacked prior history and reputation, faced high failure risk, and had highly concentrated ownership. The resulting information and incentive problems, combined with entrepreneurial private benefits of control, affect initial financing decisions. They also concluded that start-ups with high adverse selection and risk shifting problems contracted less bank debt but compensated with other debt sources. Start-ups in growing industries had lower leverage, but raised more bank debt. Entrepreneurs with large private control benefits contracted less but had longer-term bank loans to lower the default probability (pp. 143-148)

Competition intensity. This is the risk for an enterprise with intense competition: prices wars, nasty competitor behavior, and thin profit margins (Gordon, 2007). Entrepreneurial risk is diminished if there are virtually no competitors in terms of the market. When Black Entertainment Television (BET) emerged onto the cable market 1979, there was no cable television programming for Black (African American) audiences. BET followed on a growth strategy that specifically targeted Black audiences with their programming. BET, led by Robert Johnson, made an historic mark in the cable television programming. With a defined niche, Johnson had minimal risk in terms of competitors in this market. BET was practically a monopoly. Following one of the many axioms in marketing theory, as Johnson stated BET could not be all things to all people (Pulley, 2004). The risk of competition in the market place is a critical concern in terms of entrepreneurial risk. Invariably, an enterprise is at risk when there is a significantly high number of competitors in the market sector (Black, 1999; Brandenburger & Nalebuff, 1997; Buffett & Clark, 1997; Hirschey & Pappas, 1992; McAuley, 1986; Porter, 1985; Porter, 1989; Shane, 2008). There were further studies on competition (Lambing & Kuehl, 2007; Miles, & Darroch, 2006; Mossi, 1986).

Business climate/economic location. This measures the business climate in which the enterprise functions. There are higher risks involved with the business enterprise that are located in a depressed economic climate. Does the business have proximity to an economic anchor (e.g., military base, college/university, hospital, major sports facility/stadium, amusement/theme park)? Porter (1989) theorized the major characteristics of declining economic locations and industries: (a) demographics, shrinkage in the size of the customer group that purchases the product; (b) shifts in needs, demand that falls because of sociological or other causes of change in buyers' needs or tastes; and (c) lack of economic clusters (Blakely & Bradshaw, 2002; Lowenstein, 1995; Mariotti, 2007; McAuley, 1986; Porter, 1989; Psaltopoulos, Stathopoulou, & Skuras, 2005; Slater, 2003). As businesses leave the economic location, so does the business activity.

Runyan's (2005) study examined small downtown business districts and the businesses within each respective district. Runyon employed a resource-based theory to put forward a model that would identify resources available in downtown areas. He posited that downtown businesses have two separate types of resources at their disposal: business resources and structural resources. Business resources are manifest in downtown businesses, while structural resources are created by the downtown (or community) itself. When utilized, these resources have a positive effect on the downtown's success. Further studies on the business climate in downtown and urban locations for small businesses were conducted by Bates (2006), Miles, (2006), and Runyan and Huddleston (2006).

Government regulation constraints. This measures the risk of government regulation constraints on the business enterprise. This risk factor may involve significant costs of licensing and permits. Firms must deal with regulation constraints at the local, state, and federal levels. Regulation acts as both a constraint to profitability and as a protective device as barriers to entry. An antithetical example of government regulation constraints is *legislation risk*, which considers that a law might or might not be passed to protect a patent or license for a product (Dollinger, 1999). Legislation risk might also come from legislation that affects the current way of doing business for an incumbent SME. An example of legislation risk would be if a new city ordinance was passed that prohibits a business (e.g., adult-oriented businesses) from conducting business in a certain market area of the community (e.g., schools, churches) or at all (Ahwireng-Obeng & Mokgohlwa, 2002; Dollinger, 1999; Miles, 2006; Phillips & Garman, 2005).

Social responsibility risk. This measures the significant positive or negative impact of the business on the law enforcement, community, neighborhood, environment, and nation. Certain business enterprises arouse negative attention from these organizations, which may affect profits. Adult-oriented businesses may arouse negative attention from law enforcement. Costly legal expenses are incurred to retain attorneys for defense in court. Thus, negative attention hurts profits. For example, Konosuke Matsushita, once stated that a business must benefit society through its actions. When a business fails to benefit society, it no longer makes money (McInerney & White, 2000).

Business environment risk forces. Business environment risks are factors of the environment, which affect profitability. These factors can have an effect on the success or failure of SMEs.

Environment/climate. This risk affects SMEs profitability due to potentially harmful weather conditions. An example of this is the Hurricane Katrina disaster in August, 2005. Not only were peoples' homes destroyed, but numerous businesses were also affected (Miles, 2006). Runyan (2006) examined how small businesses respond to nature disasters. Another example is how Hurricane Katrina and its aftermath caused small business owners in the U.S. Gulf region to experience each of these. The findings of the study concluded that nature disaster issues that affect small business were: lack of planning by small business; vulnerability to cash flow interruption; lack of access to capital for recovery; problems caused by federal assistance; and serious infrastructure problems impeding recovery.

Security risk. This risk includes the influence of crime and security issues that impacts profitability. There is high risk involved with the business enterprise that does not have security of its assets, both physical property and intellectual property. Examples are espionage, fire, vandalism, and damage from storms (Miles, 2006; Porter, 1989; Shane, 2008). Bates & Robb (2008) argued that crime's impact may be harmful, however, firms most negatively affected by crime did not appear to be less viable than identical firms that reported crime; those firms stated crime had no effect on their businesses.

Insurance protection. Insurance is available for some financial losses but cannot provide coverage against all losses such as loss in profits due to a decrease in sales or an increase in competition (Gahin, 1967; Hollman & Mohammad-Zadeh, 1984; Lambing & Kuehl, 2007; Petrakis, 2005a). However, Newman (2007) examined how entrepreneurs "endogenized" entrepreneurial risk by allowing for optimal insurance contracts. The conclusions of the study indicated that: (a) moral hazards prevented full insurance; (b) as an agent's wealth increased, so did risk; and (c) workers possessed more wealth than entrepreneurs, even under decreasing risk aversion due to tough circumstances (Newman 2007; Petrakis, 2004; Strotman 2007).

Energy/fuel risk. This affects SMEs profitability due the influence of rising fuel and energy costs (along with inflation). There is high risk involved with the business enterprise that cannot freely adjust their pricing freely with rising costs in energy and fuel costs. The 1970s were an era of rising inflation and the energy crisis. As a result of the economic activity from 1973 to 1979, caused the price of oil to rise from below $3 a barrel to over $35. This not only caused government-mandated conservation measures; but also a negative effect on the profit margins of energy-dependent firms in transportation-type industries (airlines, transit firms, distribution, shipping firms, etc.). When prices are rising rapidly, businesses cannot estimate their future costs or the value of future inventories. Thus, they became reluctant to launch new enterprises or hire new employees. From a marketing perspective, this caused more firms to attempt to predict their customers' *"pain points"* (the effects of pricing on the consumption of goods and services (Ayers, 2007; Buffet & Cunningham, 2001; Leeb & Strathy, 2006).

Terrorism risk. This affects the profitability of SMEs by the influence of a terrorist act. Many businesses failed because of the terrorist act of September 11, 2001, and its effect on some industries. Two of the industries that were most affected by the 9/11 attack were the *tourism industry* and *airline industry*. This had short- and long-term effects on the state, national, and global economy. The tourism travel industry has been one of the most impacted industries. United States tourism has not fully recovered from 9/11 (Bonham, Edmonds, & Mak, 2006; Miles, 2006; Moss, Ryan, & Moss, 2006).

Globalization risk. Globalization risk is defined as the probability of loss due to international influences. This affects SMEs profitability due the strong influence of global competition. The high risks involved with the entry of global and transnational firms into the local market place can be devastating (Acs, 1992; Ball et al., 2006; Caracelli & Greene, 1997; Shane, 2008; Slater 2003; Spector, 2003; Taylor & Smalling-Archer, 1994; Trimble, 1990). Entry into global markets creates new opportunities for exports, but there is the problem of firms' vulnerability to foreign tariffs and import restrictions (Sull, 2005).

Global competition. The risk of global competition is a significant risk factor for an enterprise. An inevitable consequence of the expansion of global marketing activity is the growth of competition on a global basis (Keegan & Green, 1997). In terms of industry after industry, global competition is a critical factor affecting success or failure. Global competition raises the bar in terms of product quality and customer value. For example in the detergent industry, Colgate, Unilever, and Procter & Gamble dominate an increasing number of detergent markets in Latin America and the Pacific Rim. Another example is the automobile industry. The industry has become fiercely competitive. In the United States, foreign automobile manufacturers such as Volkswagon, Nissan, and Toyota have discovered a demand for their cars in the United States. One critical component is that *global innovation* causes other manufacturers to meet new standards. Global competition has influenced innovations and technical advances developed outside of the United States: radial tires, anti-lock brakes, fuel injection (Keegan & Green, 1997). Global competition raises the bar to the detriment of the domestic firms' ability to meet the standard.

Porter (1990) underscored the principles of competing internationally has on firms. The pattern of international competition differs from industry to industry. At one end of the spectrum there is a form of international competition called *multidomestic*, the international industry is a collection of domestic industries. Thus, there is no issue of *national advantage or international competitiveness.* However, on the other spectrum of international competition of the industries are *global industries*; this is when a firm's competitive position in one nation significantly affects its position in other nations. Global industries by contrast are the battlegrounds, which firms from different nations in ways that affect economic prosperity. Thus, global industries are compelled to compete on internationally to achieve or sustain their competitive advantage in industry segments. (pp. 55-57)

A significant downside of global competition is its impact on the producers of goods and services. Global competition has definite characteristics of Schumpeter's theory of *creative destruction.* Global competition and innovation creates value for customers (better product and at a lower price), however it tends to destroy the domestic market and threaten the domestic firms (Keeegan & Green, 1997). The market is never static; competition is not static. As you might expect, global competition *will never be* static. The risk of global competition in the market place is a critical concern in terms of entrepreneurial risk.

National competitive advantage. For a firm to be competitive in a global environment there are determinants of competitive advantage for national firms over global firms. According to Porter (1990), the presence of particular attributes in individual countries influences industry development. Porter identified four determinants of a national competitive advantage: (a) *factor conditions,* (e.g. human resources, physical resources, knowledge resources, capital resources and infrastructure resources); (b) *demand conditions*, (e.g., composition of home demand, size and pattern of growth of home demand, rapid home market growth, means by which nation's products and services are pushed or pulled into foreign countries); (c) *related and supporting industries* (e.g., a nation has an advantage when it is home to internationally competitive industries in fields that are related to or direct support of other industries); and (d) *firm strategy, structure, and rivalry* (e.g. differences in management styles, organizational skills, and strategic perspective create advantages and disadvantages for firms competing in different types of industries). The four determinants of competitive advantage can help national firms maintain a competitive position against global competition.

Categories of globalization risk. There are generally five broad categories of globalization risk with expansion into foreign markets: (a) *cultural risk,* the probability of loss because of product market differences due to distinctive social influences or customs in foreign markets; (b) *currency risk,* the probability of loss due to swings in the relative value of domestic currency of foreign market, which are highly unpredictable in volatile markets; (c) *government policy risk,* the probability of loss due to foreign government grants of monopoly franchises, tax abatements, and favored trade status; (d) *expropriation risk,* the danger that business property owned abroad might be seized by the host government; (e) *transnational competition risk,* the possibility of loss for a firm if a multi-national firm enters the local market and competes with the local and domestic firms. Multi-national firms are often strong competitors on price due to the competitive advantage of exploiting both their multi-national and transnational capabilities (e.g., cheap labor costs, access to resources, lower manufacturing costs) (Ball et al., 2006; Hirschey, 2006; Zacharakis,1997).

In terms of global marketing, the issue of customer value is tied to the sourcing decision. The risk here is that if foreign customers are nationalistic, they may put a positive value on the feature "made in the home country." Keegan & Green (1997) argued that six sourcing decisions are one of the most complex and important decisions faced by a global company: *factor costs and conditions* (e.g. labor, land materials, and capital costs); *country infrastructure* (e.g. important if a country's infrastructure be sufficiently developed to support an operation); and *exchange rate, availability, and concertibility of local money* (e.g. the cost of production supplied by a country sources will be determined by the prevailing foreign exchange rate for the country's currency).

Sull (2005) asserted that many dominant Western companies, such as Microsoft and Wal-Mart have found China a difficult market to crack due to globalization entry barriers. There were other risk factors that make entering China difficult: intellectual property protection, regulatory obstacles, and distribution bottlenecks. Succeeding in China is difficult. Other globalization risk concerns are:

(a) *commercial risk* refers to the buyer's ability to pay for the products or services ordered; (b) *foreign currency risk* refers to the situation when a company bills in a currency other than its own; which can be devalued by market fluctuations; (c) *transfer risk* refers to the probability of loss due to a foreign customer's delay in payments from bureaucracies from the foreign exchange rate market controls; and (d) *political risk* refers to the occurrence of war, revolutions, local government corruption, assassinations, political executions, limits of foreign ownership, instability of government infrastructure, insurgencies, or civil unrest. (Jeannet & Hennessey, 2001, pp. 424-426)

Di Gregorio (2005) concluded that established measures of *country risk* were unreliable predictors of actual volatility although country risk analysis is a well-established field within international business. Conventional strategies aimed at minimizing or otherwise avoiding downside risk were likely to yield limited results at best. At worst, these strategies would lead managers to miss entrepreneurial opportunities, which were likely to be greatest during conditions of disequilibrium. Strategies may be devised to harvest upside volatility while containing downside volatility by focusing on both the downside and upside elements of country risk. Rather than being something to avoid, country risk has become an opportunity to profit from uncertainty (Barker, 1992; Di Gregorio, 2005; Yamada, 2004).

Kotler & Keller (2009) identified six market entry concerns for SME firms understanding markets and the marketing environment (also *foreign markets*). These are macro-environmental trends and forces that have an influence on the market. SMEs. *Demographic environment* is concerned with population growth, population age mix, ethnic markets, educational groups, household patterns, and geographical shifts in population. *Economic environment* is concerned with income distribution and savings, debts, and credit availability. *Socio-political environment* is concerned with high persistence of core values (e.g., view of themselves, others, organization, society, nature, and universe); and the existence of subcultures. *Natural environment* is concerned with corporate environmentalism, and environmental trends (e.g., shortages of raw materials, increased cost of energy, increased pollution levels and role of changing governments). *Technological environment* is concerned with technology's influence that shapes people's lives (e.g., pace of technological change, opportunities for innovation, research and development budgets, and regulation of technological change). *Political environment* is concerned with business legislation and growth of special-interest groups (e.g., consumer movements) (Kotler & Keller, 2009).

Technology risk. This affects SMEs in terms of technological influences that might cause a business to fail because of a change in technology. Following the Schumpeter's (1942/1975) theory on *creative destruction* in the context of technology, Christensen (1997) argued that "historically firms that led in launching *disruptive technology* (products) together generated a cumulative total of $62 billion in revenues between 1976 and 1994. Those that followed into markets later after those markets had become established, logged only $3.3 million in total revenue" (pp.130-131). Through this observation, he penned the concept, "The Innovator's Dilemma" the concept of disruptive technology and innovation used in business and technology literature to describe innovations that improve a product or service in ways that the market does not expect (Christensen, 1997).

Furthermore, firms that sought growth by entering small, emerging markets generated 20 times the revenues of the firms pursuing growth in larger markets. The difference in revenues per firm is even more striking: the firms that *followed* late into markets enabled by disruptive technology generated an average of cumulative total of $64.5 million per firm. On the other hand, the average company that *led* in disruptive technology generated $1.9 million in revenues. This is an *innovators dilemma*. Christensen further argued that companies have exchanged a *market risk* (the risk that an emerging market for the disruptive technology might not develop after all) for a *competitive risk* (the risk of entering markets against entrenched competition) (p. 132).

In a refined definition of creative destruction, McInerney and White (2000) discussed the concept of *dematerialization*, "Whenever cheaper information is substituted for material inputs like labor and natural resources, large parts (eco-systems) of the industry are literally 'dematerialized' and cease to exist" (p. 139). The impact of dematerialization is devastating to industrial (legacy) firms. For example, once the capability of delivering music via the Internet was available, the need for products like the compact discs (CD) simply disappeared. When dematerialization happens, entire industries are devastated; the entire industry that used to manufacture, package, publish, distribute and deliver those products has now become obsolete. This means no record stores. Thus without record stores, traffic and buying patterns in many large shopping malls must also change.

For example, the effect of dematerialization has been disastrous to the Kodak Corporation. In Kodak's case, the emergence of the digital camera eliminated the core of their primary revenue streams. In the case of Kodak, dematerialization eliminated the need for three inputs were (a) film, (b) film processing, and (c) film-processing products (e.g., paper and chemicals). The core of Kodak's revenue streams were based on those three inputs; and they were all destroyed with the advent of digital cameras, cell phone digital cameras, in-home laser printers and Internet photographs made available to relatives and friends (McInerny & White, 2000). The threat of dematerialization permeates nearly all legacy industries. This is most evident in the music industry.

An example of another creative destruction concept that has emerged most recently in the music industry is the trend of *deintegration*. Deintegration is the act of focusing on two to four steps in the value chain. In the deintegration pattern, value shifts from strategic control by a few integrated producers to domination of only one or two steps along the *value chain* (inbound logistics, operations, outbound logistics, marketing & sales, and service) by an emerging group of specialists.

A classic example of this concept is Apple Corporation. Surprisingly, Apple Corporation took advantage of *both* strategies of dematerialization and deintegration:

> Apple Corporation's, sale of digital music through their proprietor platforms, iTunes and the iPod, has both *dematerialized* and *disintermediated* the entire music industry. Because of growth of both iTunes and the digital music sales, the traditional music retailer's business model (physical inventory and sales of CDs) has literally been destroyed. (Knopper, 2009, pp. 171-215)

Slywotzky, Morrison, Andelman, Moser, Mundt, and Quella (1999) discussed this emerging trend in 1970s. For the past several decades, the *vertically integrated business models* dominated many major industries. This is illustrated with companies who dominated this by controlling the value chain; thus by also trying to control many things *within* the value chain. This has involved such industries as steel, chemicals, auto, airline, computing, textiles, plastics, aerospace, banking, consumer package goods, publishing, oil and gas, and pulp and paper.

Interestingly, the disintegration trend emerged in the 1970s. New competitors emerged as value chain specialists in those industries. For example, Intel, Nucor Microsoft and Creative Artists Agency emerged during the 1970s. Many of the dominant legacy companies in the old vertical integration paradigm that tried to do too many steps in the value chain eventually failed. Those firms that emerged during the 1970s illustrated the trend of deintegration. By contrast, new firms began to realize they can focus on three or four steps of the value chain. Deintegration involves outsourcing, deregulation, and specialization (Slywotzky et al., 1999).

From a *creative destruction* (Schumpter, 1975) perspective, the emergence of dematerialization and disintermediation in the music industry has: (a) caused the collapse of the traditional supply chain infrastructure, from which album and compact discs (CD) sales were generated; (b) eliminated the need for physical record stores, and caused major retailers such as Camelot, Virgin Megastores, Tower Records, and others to go out of business; and (c) caused major big box retailers such as Wal-mart, Best Buy, Borders, and others to drastically reduce shelf space of CDs (Knopper, 2009 p. 161). From a profit margin perspective, digital music sales (MP3s) are potentially more profitable than CDs ever were; they carry no overhead expenses of warehouses, crates, shipping and record stores. Due to dematerialization and disintermediation, the recorded music industry has been declining and will continue to decline

(Knopper, 2009). Although this paradigm shift in the music industry is great for consumers, it is a negative for the music industry. "In this post-era of iTunes, record labels had to lay off thousands of people and cut all but the obvious big-selling acts from their artist rosters" (Knopper, 2009, p. 175).

McKnight, Vaaler, and Katz (2001) extended Schumpeter's creative destruction theory (1942/1975) by offering four basic concepts that affect both traditional and technology firms in terms of technological risk:

> (a) *the destruction of traditional industry structures*, when clearly defined industry boundaries, entry barriers, and market position within a traditional industry have been replaced by the introduction of new technologies and innovations; (b) *the destruction of traditional regulatory approaches*, when regulatory frameworks or government regulation limit competitive entry and the established monopoly that incumbent firms benefited from [*sic*]; (c) *the destruction of traditional competitive positioning strategies*, when persistently profitable, protected market positions have been replaced by "hypercompetitive" strategies; and (d) *the destruction of traditional technological assumptions*, when historical dominance of analog, narrow bandwidth, and related technologies designed primarily for voice-telephony were being displaced by digital, wireless, and IP-based platforms. (pp. 14-16)

Sull (2005) offers another refined definition of the *creative destruction* concept, referred to as *sudden-death threats*. Sudden-death threats are major environmental shocks that threaten an established firm's business with extinction. Sudden-death threats challenge a firm's ability to create, and capture, and sustain value. For incumbent firms, simply sensing and anticipating emerging opportunities and threats is not enough; firms must translate their insight into effective action.

Product life cycle. Earlier research shows that entrepreneurial risk may also be attributed to the location of a SME within the product life cycle (e.g., introduction, growth, maturity, or decline phases). For example, a SME in the decline phase may experience an industrial technological change due to the emergence of a new technological process (*"disruptor technology"*); as in the conversion from analog video recording methods (VHS) to digital techniques (DVD). This situation would make VHS manufacturers obsolete, while DVD manufacturers would prosper. This is an example of disruptor technology (Christensen, 1997; McInerny & White, 2000; McKnight, Vaaler, & Katz, 2001). Changes in markets, industries and technology were mentioned earlier in the literature review illustrating Schumpeter's (1975) theoretical concept of "creative destruction."

This assertion is supported by Barker's (1992) theory on paradigms that stated that all firms and industries go through a *paradigm shift*, a pattern that transpires when changes emerge in the industry. Consequently, firms that were once dominate in the *old paradigm* are no longer dominate in the *new paradigm*; thus they have to start over or *"return to zero"* to remain competitive. Those characteristics are similar in declining economic communities. There is significant entrepreneurial risk if the enterprise competes in a declining industry or operates in a declining economic location. Nevertheless, a practice of avoiding entrepreneurial risk involves screening ventures and eliminating unnecessary processes for reaching the customer.

Business and industry classification by market saturation. In an interesting characteristic of Warren Buffet's investment philosophy concerning business risk was his dislike of competition. He has a unique classification of businesses and industries (Buffett & Clark, 1997; Lowenstein, 1995; Train, 1980). Considering there are over 19 major sectors of 2-digit industries that are classified by North American Classification System (NAIC), however, Buffett classifies businesses in industries by a much simpler method: by their level of *risk* and *competition intensity*. This is based on *market saturation*. Buffett refers to these types of businesses or industries with *commodity-characteristics*; the end consumer does not distinguish between *suppliers of raw materials* (e.g., corn, bananas, and beef) or *manufacturing businesses of common goods* (e.g., screws and bolts, tools, and component parts). The end customer did not know they *existed*. Based on Buffett's framework, he classifies industries in three general categories: (a) consumer monopoly-type industries; (b) consumer competitive-type industries; and (c) commodity-type industries.

Consumer monopoly-type industries. These are businesses in industries that have little to no competition; they are monopolistic and have a strong identifiable niche. Price is not an important consideration to the consumer; because they are willing to pay the firm's asking price for their product regardless of cost. This is a business that has great economics, companies for which you can reasonably predict future income. Warren Buffet refers to consumer-monopoly type businesses as *"toll bridge businesses."* The "toll bridge" is a classic form of a consumer monopoly. For example, if the consumer wants to cross a river without swimming or using a boat, they very likely have to cross on a bridge and *pay the toll*. An overwhelming characteristic of consumer monopoly-type businesses is that they tend to have a strong *competitive advantage*. Another characteristic is that they attempt to convince consumers to purchase on the basis of *brand*, rather than *price* (Buffett 2001; Buffett & Clark, 1997; Clemens, 2006; Lowenstein, 1997; Slywotzky, Morrison, & Andelman, 2002).

Consumer competitive-type industries. These are industries that have few competitors, but are not monopolistic and have a strong identifiable niche in the marketplace. *Brand-affiliated businesses* are typically retail businesses. Their existence tends to be known by consumers. Price is not an important consideration; but market position is important. They have a strong competitive advantage important (Buffett & Clark, 2001).

Commodity-type industries. These are businesses that sell a product or service where price is the single most important motivating factor in the consumer's buying decision. These tend to be businesses indistinguishable from their competitors. Examples are textile manufacturers, producers of raw materials such as corn and rice, steel producers, gas and oil companies, lumber industry and paper manufacturers. All these companies sell a commodity for which there is a considerable amount of competition in the marketplace. For example, one buys gasoline on the basis of price, not on the basis of brand. In the commodity-type business, the low-cost provider wins. The product or services in these types of industries do not have any defining characteristics to the consumers. The consumer cannot distinguish between firms' products or services nor do they have an identifiable competitive advantage. Market position is not important (Buffett 2001; Buffett & Clark, 1997; Fridson, 2000; Lowenstein, 1997). A further defined example is illustrated in the retail part of the supply chain with the commodity product, bananas. When a consumer purchases bananas at a retailer (grocery store), they shop at a retailer on the basis of product, not on the basis of brand. With commodity-based goods, a consumer shops for *bananas*, they generally do not shop for "Dole Bananas" or "Chiquita Bananas" (Buffett, 2001; Buffett & Clark, 1997; Lowenstein, 1997).

Franchising as an alternative. One of the forms of entrepreneurship is franchising. Franchising has emerged as an alternative and has become competitive as an option. However, franchising is not a silver bullet to business success; franchising has risk. Franchises can and do fail (Michael & Combs, 2008). Franchising is considered an action of *risk minimalization*, thus less risky than engaging in a new venture start-up enterprise. The franchising concept consists of two components: franchisor and franchisee. The *franchisor* owns the franchise entity or concept and sells the concept to interested parties (franchisee) for a fee. The *franchisee* purchases and owns the rights to use the trademarks, patents, and legal control from the franchisor. Historically, franchise failure rates were substantially below the failure rates for new businesses in general (Cavaliere & Swerdlow, 1988; p. 10). The franchise trait is one of several determinants of survival prospects (Bates, 1998).

There are advantages to franchising that limit entrepreneurial risk. *Technical and administrative support* is the comfort and security obtained for new business owners from working within a framework of a franchise. *Shared risk* is the reduced and minimized through *risk sharing* in a quasi-structured environment. *Brand equity* is the benefits of the franchiser's name recognition, network, systems, training, and infrastructure to help establish and grow their business. *Lesser constraints to capital* is the financing that is more easily obtained from a franchisor than from other sources. *Transition ease* is the individuals' transition ease from corporate life to business ownership (Selig, 1998; p. 13).

Sherman (1999) made a compelling argument that aspiring entrepreneurs should consider franchising as opposed to the risk of a start-up venture. Historically, franchising has been highly competitive and saturated with fast-food industries. However, franchising has expanded into to other industries: energy services, healthcare, consulting, financial services, and other industries. There is a misconception concerning the success of franchises. Overall most franchises do succeed; however, *franchises do fail* (Michael & Combs, 2008). Two components play a critical role in the success or failure of a franchise: the *franchisor* and *franchisee*. Franchises are successful due to the several factors:

> *Age* is the experience gained over time and thus is a relevant factor. *Experience* is gained when the franchisors are likely to become more adept at identifying desirable unit locations and qualified franchisees. *Improvement of the concept* is the experience gained from the franchisor's experience with goods or services costs, which will likely to decline as the company grows and pass the cost reductions on to the franchisees. *Environmental conditions* are the specific exogenous conditions are faced by all competitors within a particular industry. (Castrogiovanni, Justis, & Julian, 1993, p. 105)

Shane and Foo (1999) conducted research on franchise survival. They conducted a longitudinal study on the survival of 1,292 new franchisors established in the U.S. from 1979-1996. The results of their study revealed: (a) *newer franchisors* were more likely to fail, (b) *smaller franchisors* were more likely to fail, (c) *franchisors from registration states* (e.g., states that require registration and approval of the franchise documents prior to selling in the state or from the state) were more likely to fail if they had greater capitalization, (d) franchisors with external certification were less likely to fail, and (e) *franchisors from termination states* (e.g., states with laws that govern franchise relationships in cases of termination by the franchisor to the franchisee) were less likely to fail if they use franchising more heavily. Based on the literature, it has been substantiated that franchises bear a fewer number of risk factors compared to a start-up ventures. However, it would be inaccurate to state that franchises are not risk; franchises are *less* risky (pp. 142-159).

Selection of Variables

Table 2 shows the five a priori risk factors and the items within each factor.

Table 2. Summary of Entrepreneurial Risk Factors

Factors	Variables
Personal Characteristics Risks	(a) age, (b) gender, (c) education, (d) ethnicity, (e) length of business ownership, (f) expertise in industry/field, and (g) income.
Intangible Operation Risks	(a) business entity type, (b) capital investment intensity, and (c) time intensity dependence.
Enterprise Operations Risks	(a) labor/operating costs, (b) equipment/systems investment, (c) diseconomies of scale/ Internet, (d) protection mechanisms, (e) intellectual capital, (f) velocity of profit, and (g) customer turnover/turnaround.
Market Climate Risks	(a) market potential, (b) market entry/exit barriers, (c) competition intensiveness, (d) business climate/economic location, (e), government regulation constraints, (f) social responsibility, and (g) social risks.
Business Environment Risks	(a) environment/climate, (b) security risk, (c) terrorism risk, (c) inflation/energy/fuel costs, and (d) globalization risk.

Rationale for selection of variables. Every measureable risk factor included in the instrument was referenced from the review of the literature. The decision of the researcher for choosing risk variables to include was determined by the ease of measurability. Some risk variables could not be reasonably measured for this study.

Table 3 shows the literature sources for each item of the ERAS instrument. The table shows each item and some of its sources. The items listed from 1 to 13 indicate the demographic components of the instrument. The items listed from 14 to 37 indicate the risk factor variables to be measured for the study. The majority of the risk variable items in the ERAS instrument were developed to measure specific characteristics of entrepreneurial risk of enterprises.

Table 3. Literature Sources for ERAS Instrument Development

Item	Sources
1. Gender	Browne, 2001; Collins, 2007; Robb, 2002; Shane, 2008
2. Marital status	Shane, 2008
3. Children in household	Subject Matter Expert Panel-1
4. Current age	Shane, 2008
5. Level of education	Shane, 2008
6. Ethnicity	Robb, 2002; Shane, 2008
7. Wages/salary from the enterprise	Miles, 2006; Shane, 2008
8. Industry type or market sector of business	Buffett & Cunningham, 2001; Phillips & Garman, 2005;
9. Length of time owning business/industry experience	Miles, 2006
10. Industry experience	McCormack, 1984; Shane, 2008; Stanley, 2001; Trump & Schwartz, 1987
11. Business enterprise (startup or franchise)	Subject Matter Expert Panel-2
12. Number of employees	Subject Matter Expert Panel-2; Ball, 2006; Bygrave, 1994
13. Professional licensing	Subject Matter Expert Panel-2
14. Business entity type	Kennedy, 2005; Lechter, 2001; Miles, 2006; Sutton, 2001
15. Capital invested into business	Bartlett, 1999; Berkery, 2008; Formani, 2001; Giles & Blakely, 2001; Kennedy, 2005; Lechter, 2001; Miles, 2006; Shane, 2008; Sutton, 2001

Table continues

Table 3 (continued)

Item	Sources
16. Negative attention or public relations with the business (or business model).	Miles, 2006
17. Weather conditions of business area.	Miles, 2006
18. Crime levels of business area	Miles, 2006; Porter,1998; Shane, 2008
19. Terrorism vulnerability of business location/economic area.	Miles, 2006
20. Price adjustment ability due to inflation or increase in energy costs.	Buffet & Cunningham, 2001; Leeb & Strathy, 2006; Miles, 2006;
21. Threat of market entry and competition with dominant competitors in local market	Ball et al., 2006; Shane, 2008; Slater 2003; Spector, 2003; Taylor & Smalling-Archer, 1994;
22. Business' sole dependency on owner for profitability	Kiyosaki & Lechter, 1999
23. Labor intensity level	Miles, 2006
24. Overhead costs	Shane, 2008
25. Investment in equipment, systems or technology	Dollinger, 1999; Miles, 2006
26. Internet technology use	McInerney & White, 2000; Miles, 2006; Subject Matter Expert Panel-2
27. Team of experts for advice	Gerber, 1995; Sutton, 2003
28. Intellectual capital and property protection	Sutton, 2003; Sutton, 2001
29. Customer payments/velocity of profits	Miles, 2006; Thomas, 1991
30. Customer turnover/activity	Ayres, 2007; Miles, 2006;
31. Credit use by customers	Subject Matter Expert Panel-2; Dollinger, 1999
32. Line of credit with lending institution	Subject Matter Expert Panel-2 Dollinger, 1999

Table continues

Table 3 (continued)

Item	Sources
33. Market potential	Dollinger, 2002; Hirschey, 2006; Schumpter 1975; White, Sondhi & Fried, 1998
34. Entry barriers to market	Porter, 1985; Porter, 1989
35. Competition intensity in market sector	Buffett & Clark, 1997; Hirschey & Pappas, 1992; Laming & Kuehl, 2007; McCauly, 1986; Porter, 1989; Porter, 1998; Shane, 2008;
36. Economic condition of business location/area.	Bates, 1985; Blakely & Bradshaw, 2002; Lowenstein, 1995; Miles, 2006; Porter, 1998; Runyan, 2005
37. Government regulation: local, state, federal regulations required to conduct business.	Ahwireng-Obeng & Mokgohlwa, 2002

Conceptual framework of study. The conceptual framework of this study draws from the five forces of risks identified in the literature. This study specifies the proposed relationships for this study. Those five factors of entrepreneurial risk has been identified and will be investigated for this study (see Figure 1). The framework illustrates the path of causality for the entrepreneurial risk orientation. The five forces have a causal impact on firm behavior; and a direct impact on entrepreneurial risk orientation.

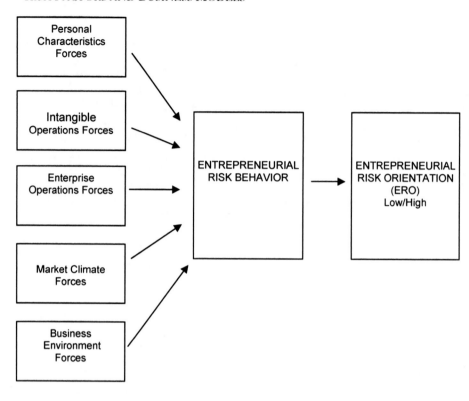

Figure 1. Conceptual framework of study model

Summary of Chapter 2

This chapter presented a review of the literature in research and theory relevant to this study on entrepreneurial risk. The chapter focused on the operationalization of different types of risk. The review examined prior studies that were directly related to entrepreneurial risk of enterprises rather than focusing on entrepreneur risk behavior.

Chapter 3, the methodology section focuses on the methods of quantitative validation of the ERAS instrument. This chapter discusses the sample, sources of data, measurement and the statistical analysis methods. The sample used for this study will be discussed in greater detail and the sources of the data will be described. Finally, the measurement of the dependent variables, independent variables, control variables and the analytical techniques will be discussed.

Chapter 3
Methodology

This chapter describes the research methods utilized in this study. The overall research design and procedural aspects were chosen based on: (a) the problem identified for investigation, (b) the purpose and overall study objectives, and (c) the guiding research question. The methodology used for this study achieved the primary objective of testing the validity of the Entrepreneurial Risk Assessment Scale (ERAS) is to measure the critical forces of entrepreneurial risk (ER) with nascent and incumbent small-to-medium business enterprises (SME).

Entrepreneurial Risk Assessment Scale (ERAS)

ERAS combines assessments of risk orientation as found in Accounting, Economics, Management, Marketing, Finance, and Entrepreneurship literature. It attempts to identify and predict entrepreneurial risk patterns in SMEs. The ERAS consists of a 37-item scale based on five factors of entrepreneurial risk found in the literature. These factors are: (a) personal characteristics; (b) intangible operations; (c) enterprise operations; (d) market climate; and (e) business environment.

Development of the Instrument. The ERAS instrument was developed from the literature to identify and predict entrepreneurial risk patterns in SMEs. The instrument was developed by the researcher based on the review of literature related to the entrepreneurial risk factors identified for the study. ERAS consists of 37-item scale based on five forces of entrepreneurial risk identified in a review of the literature. The instrument was developed specifically for the study risk of small-to-medium enterprises (SME). ERAS is a researcher developed-instrument that assesses risk behavioral characteristics. The questions were developed by the researcher to represent the five major factors identified as contributing to entrepreneurial risk in SMEs. ERAS was developed based on literature from the fields of economics, marketing, management, finance, accounting and entrepreneurship.

Scale types used in the instrument. ERAS comprised of two types of measurement scales: *nominal scale,* numbers act as labels only, indicating differences in kind (e.g., identification number); and *ordinal scale,* numbers represent rank ordering. Differences between ranks have no meaning (e.g., student standing) (Kachigan, 1986). The instrument was developed through a process that consists of 37-items comprised of six different sub-scale levels of measurement (see Table 4).

Table 4. ERAS Instrument Scale Properties and Classes

Subscale Class	Number of Questions
Class 1: Continuous (open-ended) Scale Questions	7
Class 2: Two-item Scale Questions	2
Class 3: Five-item Likert Scale Questions	22
Class 4: Five-item Multiple Choice Scale Questions	3
Class 5: Six-item Multiple Choice Scale Questions	2
Class 6: Eleven-item Multiple Choice Scale Questions	1
Total scale items	37

Variable types used in the instrument. The ERAS instrument is comprised of four types of variable responses. The first variable type is *discrete variables,* data that has a finite number of possible values (e.g., "1, 2, 3, 4, 5"; *strongly disagree* to *strongly agree*). The second variable type is *continuous variables (open-end),* data that has an infinite number of values (e.g., "how old are you?"; "how much do you earn?"). The third variable type is *nominal/categorical variables,* are data that is sorted into unordered categories (e.g., "industry type- agriculture, services or manufacturing"; "married, divorced or single"). Last, variable type are *dichotomous variables,* data that has only two response options (e.g., "yes" and "no"; "male" or "female") (Allen & Yen, 1979; DeVillis, 1991; Bryman & Cramer, 1990; Fowler, 1988; Fowler 1995; Kachigan, 1986).

Subject matter experts for instrument. ERAS was reviewed by two independent subject matter expert panels for content validity. Each panel reviewed the instrument and provided constructive feedback concerning improvements and suggestions. Those improvements were implemented into the finalized and approved version of the instrument.

Field test of instrument. ERAS was pilot-tested on 30 SMEs in a South Texas city. The data collected from the field test was used to evaluate and perfect the instrument in terms of question clarity, consistency, flow and construct before beginning the distributing the survey to the targeted population. In the process of developing and refining the ERAS instrument, a pilot study was conducted with a sample population of 202 SMEs. The pilot study was conducted with a beta version of the ERAS instrument. The pilot study was used to address issues with ERAS in terms of: (a) reliability and validity of the scales, (b) survey question clarity, (d) issues or inconsistencies with the survey questions, and (e) survey design and face validity issues of the instrument. This led to the further development of the ERAS instrument and the finalized version used for the formal study. This will be discussed more in depth later in the chapter.

The ERAS Theoretical Model

The ERAS Theoretical Model is illustrated in Figure 2. This model highlights the a priori factors and number of items within each factor measured in the study. As a result, the model proposes five factors of risk critical in influencing entrepreneurial risk.

Theory development and research. On the subject of theory development, "causal thinking, and the causal modeling that often goes with it, is probably the most prominent approach to theory construction in the social sciences theorists are often interested in understanding what causes variation" (Jaccard & Jacoby, 2010, p. 137).

Concerning the function of theory and its relationship to research, Selltiz, Jahoda, Deutsch, & Cook (1951) argued that theory is considered as the most probable or most efficient way of accounting for those findings in the light of present knowledge. Nevertheless, it is always open to revision. It is not static or a final formulation. Research, on the other hand, contributes to the development of theory; it clarifies concepts; it initiates, reformulates, and it refocuses theory. Research also can suggest new theoretical formulations or extend old ones. The relation of theory and research is one of mutual contributions (pp. 441-499).

Validating the theoretical model. Theoretically, the ERAS model will address these causes of this variation concerning risk behavior with SMEs. Figure 2. illustrates the a priori factors and number of items within each factor. Chapter 5 will discuss the comparison between the ERAS theoretical model and the conclusive factor analysis results. This will be done to understand the differences between the statistical factor loadings and the ERAS theoretical model; and to validate the structure of the theoretical model.

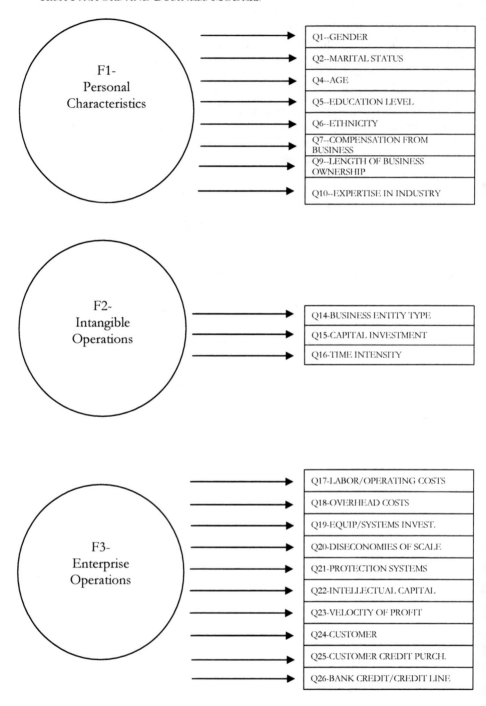

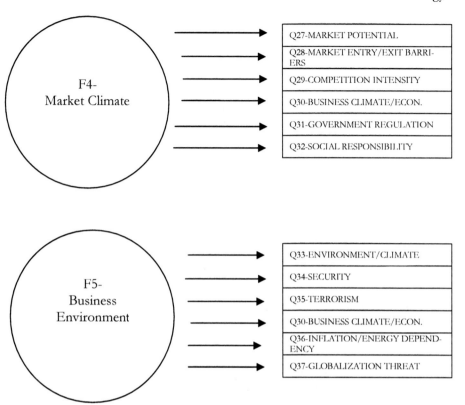

Figure 2. ERAS theoretical model

Research Design Strategy

This study used a survey research strategy. This research method gathers data from respondents who are a representative sample of a given population. Survey research often uses an instrument; it is comprised of both closed and open-ended items as a means of data collection. Historically, in the field of social sciences survey research is one of the most common forms of data collection. Some characteristics of survey research give it an advantage over other research methods. Survey research is guided by logical constraints (Allen & Yen, 1979; Babbie, 1973; Campbell & Stanley, 1963; Dunn-Rankin et al., 2004; Kish, 1987). It is deterministic; when a researcher attempts to explain the reasons for and sources of observed events (Keppel, 1982). Survey research is economical when a researcher can carefully examine the relevance of each variable. Lastly, survey research is precise (Afifi & Clark, 1984; Carlberg, 1995; Converse, & Presser, 1986; Wiersma & Jurs, 2005).

Appropriateness of design. A *cross-sectional* research design for data collection was considered most appropriate for this study. The primary function of using the cross-sectional design is the attempt to collect quantifiable data with two or more variables at a given time. This design provides a snapshot of the variables at one point in time. The selected sample should be a strong representation of the target population (Bryman, 1990; Jones, 1996; Kerlinger, 1985; Selltiz, Jahoda, Deutsch, & Cook, 1951).

Statistical analysis design. The research design also incorporated a factor analysis (FA) methodology. The factor analysis was used to provide a means of assessing validity and

reliability (Brown, 2006; Ehrenberg, 1975; George & Mallery, 2003; Kachigan, 1991; Kish,1987). FA is a multivariate statistical analysis approach that takes a large number of variables and reduces them into smaller, measurable constructs. FA is used to reduce variables to a manageable number; to identify a small number of factors representing relationships among sets of interrelated variables (e.g. descriptors); and to study relationship patterns among dependent variables (Cooper & Schindler, 2001; Gorsuch, 1983; Harman, 1976; McClave & Sincich, 2003; Mulaik, 1972; Rummel, 1970; Spearman, 1904; Walton, 1986).

An advantage of factor analysis (FA) over other statistical methods (e.g. clustering and multidimensional scaling), is it can be used to recognize certain properties of correlations to increase the interpretability of data and assist with multiple regression analysis (Aaker & Day, 1990; Darlington, Weinberg, & Walberg, 1973; Gorsuch, 1983; Kachigan, 1986; Kerlinger & Pedhazur, 1973; Kim & Mueller, 1978a; Kim & Mueller, 1978b; Rummel, 1970). However, FA is not without criticism, it has a disadvantage. One disadvantage of FA is that there are no criteria against which to test the solution in the data set; the criterion may diverge with each data set. Thus, the factors that emerge depend largely on the type of data collected (Garson, 1998; Kachigan, 1991; Kline, 1989). In other statistical methods, (e.g., discriminant analysis or regression), the solution is judged by how well it predicts group membership. However, with FA there is no external criterion by which to test the solution. FA is not a "silver bullet" (Garson, 1998; Harman, 1976; Isaac & Michael, 1985; Tabachnick & Fidell, 2007).

Data Analysis. The statistical analysis of the data was completed using three types of software. First, SAS ® (Statistical Analysis System) Version 9.1 software was used for computing the descriptive statistics, inferential statistics and multivariate statistics. This was used for establishing central tendencies (mean, median, and mode), and developing the exploratory factor analysis, and data cleaning. Multivariate statistical analysis was used for computing factor analysis (PAF and PCA), logistic regression, Pearson's Correlation, and T-tests and factor scores.

Second, SPSS ® (Statistical Package for Social Sciences) Version 17.0 software was used for computing the data from the pilot test and study. The computation included descriptive statistics, inferential statistics and multivariate statistics. This was used for establishing central tendencies (mean, median, and mode), and developing the exploratory factor analysis. Multivariate statistical analysis was computed factor analysis (PAF and PCA), logistic regression, Pearson's Correlation and T-tests. Last, SPSS ® Amos Version 6.0 (Structural Equation Modeling) software was used for developing a structural equation model for experimenting and computing a confirmatory factor analysis.

Methods Used to Establish Validity and Reliability

This research design used two types of factor analysis methods: (a) principal axis factoring (PAF) and (b) principal component factor analysis (PCA). PAF is used when the research purpose is theory confirmation and causal modeling. PCA is used when the research purpose is data reduction or exploration to a smaller number of underlying latent dimensions. PCA is not used in causal modeling. Both FA types were most appropriate for this study. The rationale for using PAF and PCA is to establish validity, conduct exploratory research, build theory, and advance theory confirmation (Bryant & Yarnold, 1995; Bryant, 2000).

    Construct validity. Construct validity indicates how well the instrument measures the theoretical concept that attempts to explain the behavior represented in the instrument. It is usually estimated by a combination of logical and empirical procedures (Bryant, 2004; Long, Convey, & Chwalek, 1985). The rationale for construct validity is to achieve *meaning* (Bryant, 2000; Garson, 1998). Construct validity has three components: (a) agreement (convergence), (b) capability to assess different things (discriminant), and (c) appearance (face) (Bryant, 2000; DeVellis, 1991; Hair, Anderson, Tatham, & Black, 1998). To establish construct validity, the researcher used principal axis factoring (PAF). Face validity is the degree to which the particular instrument appears to measure what it is intended to measure. To establish face validity, the researcher used two methods: two subject matter expert panels and a Pearson's Correlation.

    In an effort to establish construct validity further, factorial validity was also established. *Factorial validity* is the degree to which the measure of a construct conforms to the theoretical definition of the construct (Motl, Dishman, Dowda, & Pate, 2004). Factorial validity is a form of construct validity that is established through factor analysis. Factor validity is established by conducting a factor analysis on the test, in question, as well as, on a set of tests that produce known factors (marker tests). The factorial validity for the new test is exhibited by its loading on the factor. The new test's loading on the other factors should be low (Allen & Yen, 1979).

    Content validity. Content validity indicates how well the material included in the instrument represents all the possible material that could have been included. It is particularly important for achievement and proficiency measures (Bryant & Yarnold, 1995; Bryman & Cramer, 1990; Long, Convey, & Chwalek, 1985). The rationale for content validity is to achieve *thoroughness*, as a central measurement (Bryant, 2000; Garson, 1998). To establish content validity, the researcher used three methods (a) review of the literature, (b) two subject matter expert panels, and (c) a principal components analysis (PCA).

First, based on an examination of the prior literature, a study specifically focused on the subject of entrepreneurial risk is rare. A search of *Dissertation Abstracts*, using the key words "entrepreneurial risk" resulted in only 13 dissertations that either minimally examined or barely mentioned this topic. Those dissertations were from Hoff (1989), Taylor (1992), Thorne (1992) Talmachoff (1998), Gadsden (2000), Macias (2000), Neff (2004), Pardo (2005), Cunningham, (2005), Luo (2005), Wang (2006), Panousi (2008), and Roussanov (2008). However, a second search for the term "entrepreneurship" resulted in 1,387 dissertations and "risk" resulted in 64,513 dissertations.

Criterion validity. The purpose of criterion validity assesses how accurately the instrument predicts between groups, based on an established standard. The rationale was to assess the ability of the instrument to differentiate between nascent and incumbent SMEs (Bryant, 2000; DeVellis, 1991). To establish criterion validity, the researcher used a logistic regression of the factor scores obtained from the factor analysis.

Reliability. The purpose of reliability is the consistency or stability of a measure (or test) from one use to the next. To establish reliability, Cronbach alphas (α) were performed to measure the ERAS instrument's internal consistency and reliability. The key elements of reliability are internal consistency and standardization. Cronbach's Alpha is used to measure the internal consistency or reliability of a psychometric test score for items in an index. The range from 0 to 1.0 indicates how many of the items in an index measure the same thing (Vogt, 1998).

Three key elements were addressed to establish ERAS' reliability. These elements were: (a) *stability*, the reliability of a test or instrument inferred from scores through consistent results; (b) *equivalence*, the degree to which alternative forms of the same measure produce the same or similar results; and (c) *internal consistency*, the degree to which instrument items are homogeneous and reflective the same underlying constructs (Cooper & Schindler, 2001, p. 216).

Institutional Review Board (IRB) Approval

As part of the data collection process, written approval to conduct the study was obtained from the University of the Incarnate Word (UIW) Institutional Review Board (IRB). The protocol for protection of participants' rights was strictly followed. As advised by the committee chair and the university's IRB advisor, the purpose of the study, protection of anonymity and confidentiality, right of refusal, and the use of the results were explained on both the beginning and last page of the online instrument. The researcher also provided the university's IRB with samples of the instrument, recruitment letter, and a paper copy of the online version of the instrument. To follow the IRB's strict protocol of anonymity, the researcher assigned codes to the data, in lieu of, using actual names so none of the data could be used to identify individual study participants. Subsequently, the data collected for this study was secured in a locked file cabinet and will be destroyed five years after the completion of this study.

Refinements to the ERAS Instrument and Finalized Version

The finalized version of the ERAS instrument was approved by the Dissertation Committee and was pilot tested on 30 participants resembling respondents included in the formal study. The pilot test was used to assess and analyze the instrument in order to identify any issues or inconsistencies. Pilot testing is instrumental in bolstering reliability and validity (DeVillis, 1991). Fink (2006) strongly argued for the validity and necessity of pilot testing. Pilot testing has been used: (a) to anticipate actual circumstances in which the survey will be conducted; (b) to anticipate problems, and make modifications to the instrument to insure consistency and validity; (c) to check for the clarity of questions and general format of the survey; and (d) to help bolster content validity of the instrument (Fink, 2006). Prior to administering the pilot test, a pilot study was conducted with a sample population of 202 SMEs. This was conducted with a beta version of the instrument. The pilot study was used to test the reliability and validity of each of the scales. This led to the further developed of the instrument.

As a result, the pilot test was perfected from the field mistakes and instrument mistakes discovered from the pilot study. In addition, based on the feedback that the researcher received from both the pilot study participants and subject matter expert panels, the instrument was expanded. The pilot study beta instrument was expanded from a 32-item to a 37-item instrument. Five additional survey questions were added to the scale to provide a more developed instrument as a result. The final instrument also incorporated other specific suggestions from the two subject matter expert panels. Some of these suggestions included (a) rewording of some of the survey questions and statements, (b) increasing the readability of the survey directions, (c) revising the survey questions for clarity, and (d) adding questions concerning institutional credit and customer credit, and (e) adding continuous variable questions.

Population

The target population for this study was small-to-medium business enterprises (SMEs) in Bexar County (San Antonio), Texas. Bexar County has a range of industries that vary from services to construction. Table 5 illustrates the major industries in Bexar County (San Antonio). More than 50% of the industries were services, trade transportation, utilities and government. Manufacturing ranked as one of the lowest industry sectors. The population is comprised of eight major industry sectors (see Table 5).

Table 5. Major Industries in Bexar County 2007

Industry Classification	Percentage %
Services	19.0%
Trade Transportation and Utilities	18.0%
Government	18.0%
Education & Health Services	13.0%
Tourism/Leisure	12.0%
Manufacturing	7.0%
Construction	6.0%
Other Industries	5.0%

Note. The index shows the number of industries in Bexar County. Data shown is from the Texas Workforce Commission 2007. Retrieved on 2/19/2009 from http://www.co.bexar.tx.us/ED/Economy.html. Used by permission via telephone conversation on 3/24/2009.

Sample Size Determination

The sample for this study consisted of 276 small-to-medium business enterprises (SMEs), approximately 1% of the population based on an estimate of 25,456, operating in the Bexar County and San Antonio metropolitan area (Small Business Development Center (SBDC) 2007 Annual Report). The guidelines in the research literature generally state the larger the sample, the greater the accuracy (Bryman & Cramer, 1990; Cochran, 1963). For acquiring enough data to get an adequate factor analysis methodology, some researchers are stringent in their guidelines for classifying a good number of subjects in a sample: (a) 100 or fewer subjects is poor; (b) 200 subjects are adequate; (c) 300 subjects are good; (d) 500 subjects are very good; and (e) a sample of 1,000 is excellent (Huck, Cormeir, & Bounds, 1974; Hunt & Tyrell, 2001). A sample size of 200 subjects is adequate, in most cases of an ordinary factor analysis that involve a 40-item scale (Aaker & Day, 1990; Allen & Yen, 1979; DeVillis, 1991). However, a minimum sample size for a factor analysis is different. Tabachnich and Fidell (2007) advised as a general rule of thumb, it is comfortable to have a least 300 cases for factor analysis. This study nearly met the rule of thumb with a population sample of 276 cases. Failure to achieve a large sample size (100 or fewer) would make the analysis highly vulnerable to *sampling error* (Anderson, Sweeney, & Williams, 1990; Backstrom & Hursh-Cesar, 1981; Cochran, 1963; Isaac & Michael, 1982; Newton & Rudestam, 1999; Tabachnich & Fidell, 2007).

Sampling Frame

The sampling frame consisted of small-to-medium enterprises (SMEs) listed in the following databases: San Antonio 2009-2010 Yellowbook (Yellow Pages) Business section; Small Business Administration (SBA) database roster of borrowers from 2005 to 2008; Alamo City Black Chamber of Commerce membership roster; and the West San Antonio Chamber of Commerce membership roster, and personal contacts.

The researcher used the *number of employees in the enterprise* (500 or fewer) as a criterion for qualifying businesses for study inclusion. The statistical software, Statistical Package for Social Sciences (SPSS) version 17.0 generated a computerized random number from 307 pages in the Yellowbook. Each page contained approximately 360 businesses. A second random number indicated the businesses to be chosen from the yellow page directory. Businesses would then be contacted to ascertain SME status and willingness to participate.

Participation from the chambers' listings (which contained 100 to 200 different SMEs in the databases of members) were selected using a systematic sample approach. First, the businesses were screened based on the number of employees and industry. Then every third SME was selected. Participants from the SBA borrower roster were systematically selected from a database of 2,460 SME borrowers, from the 2005-2006 roster. Every seventh SME was selected. Lastly, participation from personal contacts were selected based on their convenience and accessibility to the researcher.

Data Collection Process

In the early stages of data collection, the researcher discovered the likelihood of successful participation increased significantly by carefully pre-screening and pre-calling the participants prior to administering the instrument. Due to the historically dismal response-rates and cost-prohibitive nature, the researcher made the decision against using direct-mail surveys (Beall, 2010; Leedy & Ormrod, 2001; Walton, 1986; Zikmund, 2003a; Zikmund, 2003b).

The data collection strategy progressed through four approaches: (a) *telephone cold calling*, administered the survey instrument through random phone calls to the participants from four primary listings: (a)Yellowbook (yellow pages), SBA borrowers' listing, two local chamber of commerce membership rosters, and personal contacts; (b) *web-based/email*, administration of the survey instrument via internet (Survey Monkey) following initial contact; (c) *on-site personal administered*; administered the survey instrument in-person to the participants; and (d) *drop-off surveys,* administration of the survey instrument by leaving it with the participants and making arrangements to retrieve it later.

To aid in increasing participation, the researcher reduced the paper survey from four pages to three. Participants were more likely to complete a survey with three pages as opposed to four pages. The rationale behind primarily using the Web-based and on-site surveys was attributed to prior experience gained from the conducting similar studies. These strategies proved to be a more efficient and effective method of data collection for large samples (DeVellis, 1991; Leedy & Ormrod, 2001; Zikmund, 2003a; Zikmund, 2003b).

Concerning using a random sample population, there are some obstacles that must be considered. Kish (1987) argued there are four major obstacles to randomized representation for analytic studies. First, randomized representations for analytical studies are not common because often they seem too difficult, expensive, impractical or unfeasible. Second, they face obstacles and resistance on social, moral and ethical grounds. Third, mathematical statistical difficulties pose formidable obstacles to handling exactly the double complexities of statistical analyses embedded in complex selections. Lastly, because of those theoretical difficulties, sample survey theory was developed separately from the theory of experimental designs (pp. 45-46).

Summary of Chapter 3

This chapter presented an overview and discussion of the Entrepreneurial Risk Assessment Scale (ERAS). The first section of the chapter discussed development of the ERAS instrument. The second section of the chapter reviewed and discussed the assessment of validity and reliability of ERAS. The last section of the chapter focused on discussing the project's study sample; sample size determination; research design and data collection strategy; as well as data collection procedures. Chapter 4 will describe the validation process and study results.

Chapter 4
Results of Study

The previous chapters have presented: (a) the background of the subject matter, (b) the relevant literature reviewed, and (c) the methodology of the study. The purpose of this chapter is to present the study findings. This study sought to answer the following question(s):

1. Does the Entrepreneurial Risk Assessment Scale (ERAS) provide evidence of adequate instrument validity?
2. Does ERAS provide evidence of adequate instrument reliability?

Sample Characteristics

The study collected data from 276 participants. Data was collected through the following types of collection efforts: (a) *random sample* from the local 2009 YellowBook (yellow pages) telephone directory; (b) *systematic sample* from the Small Business Administration (SBA) borrowers listing from 2002-2006; (c) *systematic sample* from the Alamo Black City Chamber of Commerce Member Directory and Westside San Antonio Chamber of Commerce Member Directory; and (d) *convenience sample* from business cards, personal and professional contacts (see Table 8).

To increase the response rate, the SME business owners (participants) were carefully screened prior to solicitation for participation in the study. All respondents were solicited via telephone ('cold-called') using the four directories and listings shown in Table 6. Subsequently, the SME owners were emailed the ERAS instrument through a Survey Monkey link (www.survey monkey.com).

Data Cleansing

After data collection was completed, a data-cleaning process was implemented prior to data analysis. When errors were detected, the original source document was located and corrected. The majority of the data-cleaning problems were of the following types: (a) data entry errors, (b) misspellings, (c) duplicate or redundancy of input, and (d) some incomplete surveys with self-reported surveys. Respondents elected to skip, or otherwise omit some questions. One of the prevailing issues with self-reported data was the participants' failure to complete the survey or skip questions altogether. Surveys with more than six skipped items were discarded. No outliers were detected.

RISK FACTORS AND BUSINESS MODELS

Table 6. Sampling Results of SME Participation in the ERAS Instrument Survey (*N* = 276)

Data Source	Sample Type	Frequency	% of Sample
YellowBook (yellow pages) directory	Random	45	16.3
SBA Borrowers listing	Systematic	58	21.0
Local Chambers of Commerce listings (2)	Systematic	64	23.1
Professional and personal contacts	Convenience	109	39.4
Total		276	100.0

In addition to double-checking surveys for missing questions (experience learned from the administering the pilot test), a considerable number of SME participants had to be recalled to complete skipped questions. If there were questions left blank, and when efforts to contact the participants were exhausted, the questions were coded as missing. After carefully examining the data, the researcher was set to begin the task of analyzing the data collected for the study.

Descriptive Statistics of Demographic Data

Descriptives of SME owners. The business owners of SMEs were asked to complete the 37-item ERAS instrument. The descriptive statistics were calculated using the Statistical Package for the Social Sciences (SPSS) version 17.0 (2008).

Table 6 shows the descriptive statistics of the sample. The majority demographics were as follows: (a) gender - 55.1% male, (b) marital status - 61.6% married, (c) education level - 29.7% baccalaureate degree, and (d) ethnicity - 46.4% Hispanic (see Table 7). There was a close parity with the variable gender (see Table 9); however, there was not a balance in terms of ethnicity, education level, and marital status.

70

Table 7. Summary of Demographic Descriptives of SME Owners

Variables	Frequency	% of Sample
Gender		
Males	152	55.1
Females	124	44.9
Marital Status		
Single (never been married)	44	15.9
Married	170	61.6
Divorced	52	18.8
Widowed	4	1.4
Separated	6	2.2
Ethnicity		
White	84	30.4
Black (non-Hispanic)	48	17.4
Hispanic	128	46.4
Other	16	5.8
Education Level		
High school diploma or less	35	12.6
Some college	113	40.9
Bachelors	82	29.7
Graduate Degree or higher	46	16.7

Descriptives of SME industry types. Table 10 presents data on the industry type of the SMEs. As indicated, the first column shows the variable; the second column shows the frequency and the third column shows the percentage of the sample. As indicated in Table 8, the descriptive statistics of the SME sample were as follows: (a) 35.5% - services industry; (b) 90.9% - non-franchises; and (c) 59.8% - had no professional license, certification, credential or other to conduct business.

Table 8. Descriptive Demographic Statistics on the Industry Types of the SMEs

Variables	Frequency	% of Sample
Industry Type		
Agriculture	3	1.1
Communications	5	1.8
Construction	26	9.4
Finance	11	4.0
Manufacturing	11	4.0
Retail Trade	34	12.3
Services	98	35.5
Technology	15	5.4
Transportation	13	4.7
Wholesale	10	3.6
Other Industry	50	18.1
Percentage of SMEs that are Franchises		
Franchises	25	9.1
Non-franchises	251	90.9
SME Respondents who Have a Professional License to Conduct Business		
License	68	24.6
Certification	33	12.0
Credential and other	10	3.6
None	165	59.8

(N = 276)

Validity and Reliability Analysis

Bryant (2000) defines *Validity* as "truth" (Bryant, 2000). In the context of multivariate statistics, validity is concerned with whether a particular conclusion is reasonable and correct. "Validity is a term to describe a measurement instrument or test that measures what it is supposed to measure; the extent to which a measure is free of systematic error" (Vogt, 1998, p. 240). Following Bryant's (2006) framework, the researcher assessed ERAS for the three types of validity: (a) construct, (b) content, and (c) criterion validity. First, construct validity was performed which included a face validity and convergent validity. Second, discriminant validity was performed. Third, content validity was performed. Lastly, criterion validity was performed.

First, a principle axis factoring (PAF) type of factor analysis (FA) was performed. The PAF was performed and resulted in a 12-factor solution of the entire ERAS instrument. The factor items were reduced from the original 37 to 30 items. The rationale for reducing the number of items was: (a) *continuous variable* items were dropped due to low factor loading coefficients below the benchmark of .3; and (b) seven items had to be eliminated from the factor analysis because they neither produced a reliable factor nor fit cognitively. The goal was to stay within the 5-factor structure of the theoretical model.

Second, another PAF was performed and resulted in a 10-factor solution. The factor items were reduced from 30 to 22 items. The rationale for reducing the number of items was: (a) *nominal variable* items were dropped due to low factor loading coefficients below the benchmark of .3; and (b) eight items had to be eliminated from the factor analysis because they neither produced a reliable factor nor fit cognitively. Again, the goal was to stay within the 5-factor structure of the theoretical model, so more FA was needed.

Last, a principle component analysis (PCA) resulted in a 5-factor solution. The factor items were reduced from 22 to 19 items. The rationale for reducing the number of items was: (a) due to low factor loading coefficients below the benchmark of .3; and (b) three items had to be eliminated from the factor analysis because they neither produced a reliable factor nor fit cognitively. The goal to stay within a 5-factor structure of the theoretical model was achieved. For this study, both factor analyses (PAF and PCA) employed a varimax rotation. Based on the results of both factor analyses, the ERAS instrument proved to be reliable.

Construct validity of 30 items. Construct validity is concerned with the central measurement issue of *meaning*. This indicates how well the instrument measures the theoretical concept assumed to explain the behavior represented in the instrument (Bryant, 2000; Kline, 1998; Long, Convey, & Chwalek, 1985; Selltiz, Jahoda, Deutsch, & Cook; 1951).

Face validity of 30 items. Face validity is concerned with the central measurement issue of *appearance*. Face validity was assessed using variables that had a previous or theoretical relationship with entrepreneurial risk orientation (ERO) behavior (DeVellis, 1991). This validity type is concerned with the relevance of the measurement instrument to what one is trying to measure is apparent "on the face of it" (Selltiz et al., 1951). Bryant (2000) argued, "face validity is purely subjective on the part of the individuals who complete or administer the instrument; on the surface it is a superficial impression" (pp. 120-121).

Subject matter expert panels. To determine face validity, the ERAS was assessed by two independent subject matter expert panels. After several modifications, ERAS was refined with the advice of: six experts in the field of entrepreneurship and business (Panel-1); and the second Panel-2 (dissertation committee). Both panels hailed from very diverse backgrounds (e.g. banking, consultants, higher education faculty). Face validity of the entrepreneurial risk factors in the ERAS was established with the assistance of a Panel-1 (see Appendix D). To evaluate the items of the survey for clarity of risk items and their relevance to small-to-medium enterprises (SME), Panel-1 was asked to rate each scale item on the instrument from "most important to least important." They then rated the transparency of the items, and the face validity of each item. Panel-2 provided comments for improvements to the scale items as well as further suggestions for necessary revisions they felt were needed to improve the instrument. Those suggestions were implemented into the final version of ERAS.

Convergent validity for 30 items. *Convergent validity* is "the degree to which multiple measures of the same construct demonstrate agreement or convergence; it is also to the degree, those measures are similar to those from other measures of the same thing" (Bryant, 2000, pp. 113-114). To establish construct validity for this study, a principal axis factoring (PAF) was performed. A factor analysis was used to assess the *convergent validity* and *discriminant validity* of the risk variables. This is to identify distinct constructs identified by unique items. This also involved the evaluation of measures against one another instead of an external criterion (Bryant, 2000; Dunn-Rankin, 1983; Garson, 1998; Kline, 1998).

Seven items were omitted, as they were nominal variables. The researcher performed a PAF on the data at interval and ratio level ERAS instrument (30 items) to reveal factor structure followed by a second factor analysis of the 22 Likert scale entrepreneurial risk items (see Table 12). To detect the underlying data structure, as explained by relationships between variables (SPSS 11.5 for Windows tutorial on factor analysis), a factor analysis was used to measure convergent validity.

In the first PAF, the Kaiser-Meyer-Olkin measure (KMO) of sampling adequacy resulted in a .744, thus above the commonly recommended value of .6; the Barlett's test of sphericity was significant $\chi^2(231) = 1067.35, p < .001$. In terms of PAF, a finding that indicators have high loadings on the predicted factors indicates convergent validity conceptually. Few items loaded into more than one factor, which indicates good discriminant validity.

Eigenvalues validity for 30 items. Eigenvalues (λ) are a statistic used in factor analysis to show how much variation in the group of variables is accounted for by a particular factor (Bryant & Yarnold, 1995; Cureton & D'Agostino, 1993; Garson, 1998; Gorsuch, 1983; Mulaik, 1972; Rummel, 1970; Tabachnick & Fidell, 2007). The standard for an eigenvalue score is greater than 1.0 (Vogt, 1993). Ten factors with eigenvalues greater than 1 were extracted which accounted for 61.54% of the variance in the 30 items tested (see Table

9). The number of factors retained was based on an examination of percentage of variance explained.

Table 9. Eigenvalues, Percentages of Variance, and Cumulative Percentages for Factors of the 30 Likert Items Entrepreneurial Risk Assessment Scale (ERAS) Questionnaire ($N = 276$)

Factor	Eigenvalue	% of Variance	% of Cumulative
1	4.49	15.49	15.49
2	2.23	7.71	23.20
3	2.01	6.93	30.14
4	1.71	5.90	36.05
5	1.48	5.12	41.18
6	1.30	4.50	45.68
7	1.23	4.26	49.95
8	1.17	4.03	53.99
9	1.11	3.83	57.82
10	1.07	3.72	61.54

Note. Extraction Method: Principal Axis Factoring

Factor loadings and communalities. The standard for coefficient loadings for a factor analysis varies depending on the type of factor analysis. Factor loadings .6 or higher are considered "high" and those below .4 are considered "low" (Jones, 1996; Garson, 1998; Hair et al., 1998; Raubenheimer, 2004). For an exploratory type of factor analysis, a .3 or higher factor loading may be acceptable. A standard for the factor coefficient loadings of .3 or higher was established for this study. Setting minimum standards for factor loadings must be interpreted based on theory, rather than arbitrary cutoff levels (Garson, 1998).

Communality (h^2) is the sum of squared loadings (SSL) for each variables across factors. It measures the percent of variance in a given variable explained by all the factors. Communality also indicates the variance which a variable has in common with other variables in the factor analysis. Communalities are valued between 0 and 1 (Bryant & Yarnold, 1995; Cureton & D'Agostino, 1993; Garson, 1998; Tabachnick & Fidell, 2007).

The standard for communalities varies depending on the type of factor analysis methodology type (PAF, PCA, etc.) sample size, and factor structure (Brown, 2006; Cureton & D'Agostino, 1993; Garson, 1998; Mulaik, 1972; Rummel, 1970). To set a standard for this study, only communality coefficients greater than .2 were considered a significant reliable indicator in the factor.

Table 10 shows the factor loadings greater than .3 for the 30 numerical items in ERAS. The PAF revealed the ERAS communality coefficients were moderate to significantly high commonalties from .207 to .787 for 28 of the 30 items. This indicates the communalities measured for this PAF met and surpassed the minimum standard for the benchmark coefficient score of greater than .2; thus were considered significant contributors to the structure. The items Q29-competition intensity and Q5-education level did not reach a factor loading greater than .3 for any factor.

In the case of the non-Likert items, Q10-industry experience and Q9-length of ownership and Q4-age loaded into one factor Maturity; Q12-number of employees and Q7-compensation loaded in a factor; and Q15-capital investment and Q7-compensation also loaded with Q15-capital investment into another factor. Taken together the researcher identified these as financial load.

Table 10. Results of 30-item Principal Axis Factoring Analysis Coefficient Factor Loadings Matrix with ERAS Risk Variables (*N* = 276)

	F1	F2	F3	F4	F5	F6	F7	F8	F9	F10	Communality
Q10-Industry Experience (b)	**.850**										**.787**
Q9-Length of Ownership (b)	**.789**										**.757**
Q4-Age (b)	**.697**										**.514**
Q16-Owner Time Dependency Risk		.587									.398
Q24-Customer/Activity Turnover		.524									.459
Q26-Line of Credit		.464					.415				.527
Q25-Customer Credit Risk		.399									.320
Q33-Environment/Climate Condition		.379		.358							.375
Q18-Overhead Cost Risk			.699								.582
Q19-Equipment Investment Risk			.652								.504
Q17-Labor Intensity			.422								.326
Q34-Security/Crime Vulnerability				.726							.585
Q35-Terrorism Vulnerability				.556	.314						.390
Q32-Social Entrepreneurship				.387							.275
Q28-Barriers to Entry					.507						.411
Q31-Government Regulation					.456						.303
Q21-Experts (Team for Advice)					.318						.363
Q30-Economic Risk					.317						.207

	F1	F2	F3	F4	F5	F6	F7	F8	F9	F10	Communality
Q12-Number of Employees (c)						**.725**					**.588**
Q7-Compensation (c)						.472	.317				**.434**
Q15-Capital Investment (c)							.536				**.385**
Q29-Competition Intensity (a)											.217
Q20-Internet/Technology								.607			.456
Q27-Market Potential Risk								.378		.310	.429
Q5-Education Level (a)											.183
Q23-Velocity of Profit									.572		.358
Q22-Intellectual Property Risk									.304		.332
Q37-Globalization Risk										.592	.429
Q36-Energy/Dependency									.344	.381	.326

Note. Extraction Method: Principal Axis Factoring;

Rotation Method: Varimax with Kaiser Normalization;

Rotation converged in 17 iterations

Factor loadings < .3 were suppressed.

(a) Items that did not load into any factor at a level greater than .3

(b) Non-Likert items grouped as maturity

(c) Non-Likert items grouped as financial load

Convergent validity of 22 Likert items. In the second PAF, five factors were extracted with eigenvalues greater than 1, which accounted for 46.37% of the variance in the 22 items tested (see Table 11). The percentage of variance explained ranged from 18.04% to 5.61% among the factors.

Table 11. Eigenvalues, Percentages of Variance, and Cumulative Percentages for Factors of the 22 Likert Items Entrepreneurial Risk Assessment Scale (ERAS) Questionnaire (*N* = 276)

Factor	Eigenvalue	% of Variance	% of Cumulative
1	3.96	18.04	18.04
2	1.95	8.87	26.91
3	1.68	7.66	34.57
4	1.36	6.18	40.76
5	1.23	5.61	46.37

Note. Extraction Method: Principal Axis Factoring

Factor loadings and communalities. Retaining five factors, every item loaded above .3 on a factor, with the exception of Q30-economic risk and Q29-competition intensity risk. These two items Q23-Velocity of profit also failed to address .2 levels of communality. Upon investigation of items in each factor, the five factors were redefined as (a) FACTOR 1 – Customer and Resources; (b) FACTOR 2 – Security risks; (c) FACTOR 3 – Operations; (d) FACTOR 4 – External Pressures; and (e) FACTOR 5 – Alternate Factors (see Table 12).

Correlation among factors. The existence of distinct factors with weak correlation among them is evidence of convergent validity, as demonstrated in the structure analysis. A Pearson's Correlation among the factors was performed to establish convergent validity. Pearson's Correlation is used to assess if there are any relationships existed between the factors in the study (Bryant, 2000; Cureton & D'Agostino, 1993; Kline, 1998). The correlations are presented in Table 13.

The Pearson correlation coefficient represents standardized covariance, for which the variance of each item is fixed to 1.00 (Bryant & Yarnold, 1995). The benchmark for a Pearson Correlation (a) $.3 < r < .5$ is considered poor, (b) $r < .5$ is considered moderate, and (c) $r > .5$ is considered strong. The correlations in Table 13 between factor scores for the five factors identified show that the factors are also distinct from one another. Correlations are low to moderate, as we would expect. There were not strong positive correlation coefficients among factors. The highest correlation on the Table 13 is $r = .455$ Customer resources and Alternate factors; the lowest was $r = .133$ between Operation and Alternate factors coefficients (see Table 13).

Table 12. Results of Principal Axis Factoring Analysis Coefficient 5-Factor Loadings Matrix with 22 Likert items of ERAS ($N = 276$)

Items	F1	F2	F3	F4	F5	Communality
Q26-Line of Credit	**.624**					.357
Q25-Customer Credit	.540					.328
Q24-Customer Activity/Turnover	.539					.367
Q16-Owner Time Dependency	.504					.242
Q21-Experts (Team of Experts Adv)	.489					.293
Q27-Market Potential	.421					.283
Q20-Internet/Technology	.402					.284
Q22-Intellectual Property	.340					.209
Q34-Security/Crime Vulnerability		**.599**				.308
Q35-Terrorism Vulnerability		.584				.300
Q33-Environment/Climate		.466				.256
Q32-Social Benefit/Entrepreneur		.393				.203
Q29-Competition Intensity						.152
Q19-Equipment Investment			**.641**			.353
Q18-Overhead Cost			.589			.350

Items	F1	F2	F3	F4	F5	Communality
Q17-Labor Intensity			.448			.227
Q37-Globabalization Risk			-.317			.165
Q31-Government Regulation				**.468**		.233
Q28-Barriers to Entry	.352			.444		.317
Q30-Economic Risk						.170
Q23-Velocity of Profit					**.572**	.198
Q36-Energy/Dependency					.407	.215

Note. Extraction Method: Principal Axis Factoring Analysis
Rotation Method: Varimax with Kaiser Normalization.
Rotation converged in 10 iterations.
Note. 5 Components Extracted; factors > .3 are in bold.

Table 13. Results of Pearson's Correlation for ERAS Factor Scores ($N = 276$)

	Factor 1: Customer and Resources	Factor 2: Security	Factor 3: Operations	Factor 4: External Pressures	Factor 5: Other and Alternate Factors
Factor 1: Customer and Resources	1.00				
Factor 2: Security	.245	1.00			
Factor 3: Operations	.211	.238	1.00		
Factor 4: External Pressures	.399	.291	.303	1.00	
Factor 5: Other and Alternate Factors	.455	.150	.133	.273	1.00

Note. All coefficients are significant at $p < 0.01$

(a) $r < .3$ is considered poor;
(b) $r = .5$ is considered moderate;
(c) $r > .5$ is considered strong (Bryant & Yarnold, 1995).

Discriminant validity of 22 Likert items. Discriminant validity is "the degree to which multiple measures of different concepts are distinct" (Bryant, 2000, p. 114). If a particular measure is truly distinct from other measures, then it should form its own separate dimension when factor-analyzed along with other measures that supposedly assess different concepts. With discriminant validity, it should not correlate highly if they are in fact valid measures of these different concepts (Bryant, 2000). In a varimax rotation of the PAF, *discriminant validity* is demonstrated when the two factors do not overlap conceptually (Campbell & Stanley, 1963; Garson, 2009). Factor scores were generated for each of the five variables in the 22 Likert Scales.

Table 13 show Pearson's correlation between factors is low; Table 13 shows loadings good to only one factor with items Q20, Q32, and Q28 showing loadings greater than .3 for two factors, but higher loadings of at least .09 greater in the strongest factor. In summary, this reveals the ERAS instrument reflects a low common measure of correlation (highest $r = .455$; lowest $r = .133$) between the X-axis and Y-axis coefficients. This indicates good discriminant validity.

Content validity for Likert items. Content validity is concerned with the central measurement issue of *thoroughness*. *Content validity* indicates how well the material included in the instrument represents all possible material that could have been included (Bryant, 2000; Kline, 1998; Long et al., 1985). To establish content validity in statistical research, the appropriate assessment used was a principal component analysis (PCA). The major reason for content validity is to achieve *thoroughness* as a central measurement issue.

Built following review of the literature. The content validity was supported from the review of the literature. Based on the dimensions of risk identified in a review of the literature, the ERAS instrument was developed from key concepts in the fields of economics, marketing, management, accounting and finance and entrepreneurship. The entrepreneurial risk orientation (ERO) factors examined for this study are inclusive of both endogenous and exogenous variables.

In addition, prior studies were a major influence on the development of the ERAS instrument. These studies were directly related to entrepreneurial risk of enterprises rather than risk personalities or risk behavior. Notable research were from scholars in the various fields of business such as Abdelsamad et al., (1978), Miles & Snow et al., (1978), Drucker (1984), Richards (1984), and Dickson & Giglierano (1986). Other notable research was conducted by Taylor (1992), Hamilton (2000), and Norton & Moore (2006)

Principal component analysis of the ERAS instrument. Using the factor structure obtained from the principal axis factoring (PAF) on 22 Likert items, a principal component analysis (PCA) was run on each set of items in a factor to identify the smallest number of factors that together account for all of the total variance in the correlation matrix of the original variables (Bryant, 2000). PCA is used when the research purpose is data reduction or exploration and when research is a variance-focused (Garson, 1998). The ERAS instrument (22 items) is used to reveal factor structure to detect the underlying structure of the data, as explained by relationships among variables (see Table 12).

The items which included the structure developed in the PAF, were entered together again in the PCA, allowing for only one component in each factor of the KMO. The loadings and communalities indicated the soundness of the structure. Table 14 shows each factor revealed only one component with eigenvalues greater than 1.00. Table 14 shows the KMO and percentage varied in one-factor loadings and communalities. This resulted in good validity to this structure. As illustrated in Table 14, the PCA factor loadings for the 20 ERO variables (Q16- Q37) excluded two items, Q29-Competition Intensity and Q30-Economic Risk. They were excluded from the PCA due to low factor loadings and communalities (Table 14).

Reliability. Cronbach alphas (α) were performed to measure internal consistency and reliability of the ERAS instrument. Cronbach's Alpha is used to measure the internal consistency or reliability of a psychometric test score for items in an index; and measures ranges from 0 to 1.0 to indicate how much the items in an index measure the same thing (Vogt, 1993). Table 15 shows alphas above .5 for all components when Q37 is removed.

There have been varying opinions concerning a benchmark for Cronbach's Alpha (α) coefficients. The Cronbach's Alpha coefficient requires a reliability of .7 or higher; other researchers argue .8 or higher (Bryman & Cramer, 1990; Morgan, Reichert, & Harrison, 2002). For the purposes of this study, a benchmark of .5 had been established for internal consistency reliability. On the other hand, the number of items in the scale has a bearing on the benchmark for the Cronbach's Alpha. In a Cronbach's Alpha, as the number of items in the scale (k) increases, the value of (α) becomes larger (George & Mallery, 2003). Historically, Cronbach's Alpha has been used to measure how well a set of items measures a single *unidimensional latent construct* (DeVellis, 1991). Unidimensionality is defined as the responses to the items placed in rank order demonstrate a cumulative relationship in a scale. The one-dimensional scaling technique *ranking scaling* was used for the ordinal properties of the measuring the data (Coleman, 2001; De Leeuw, 2004; Dunn-Rankin, 1983; Gorden, 1977; Rummel, 1970). See Table 15.

Table 14. Results of 19-item Principal Component Analysis Factors with ERAS (*N* = 276)

Factors	KMO	Eigenvalues	% of Variance	Factor Loading	Communality
Customer and Resources					
Owner Time Dependency	.736	2.168	43.35	.718	.411
Customer Activity/Turnover		.882	17.64	.677	.516
Customer Credit Risk		.762	15.23	.656	.431
Line of Credit		.613	12.26	.641	.458
Market Potential Risk		.575	11.49	.594	.352
Security					
Security/Crime Vulnerability	.693	1.854	46.34	.749	.560
Terrorism Vulnerability		.810	20.23	.729	.532
Environment/Weather Risk		.736	18.39	.619	.383
Social Responsibility/Entrepreneurship		.601	15.01	.616	.379
Operations					
Overhead Cost	.621	1.753	58.44	.816	.448
Equipment Investment Risk		.743	24.77	.799	.666
Labor Intensity		.504	16.78	.669	.639
External Pressures					
Barriers to Entry	.578	1.545	51.51	.798	.435
Government Regulation Risk		.837	27.91	.688	.637
Internet/Technology Use		.617	20.57	.660	.473

Factors	KMO	Eigenvalues	% of Variance	Factor Loading	Communality
Other and Alternate Factors					
Intellectual Property Risk	.631	1.644	41.09	.709	.502
Experts for Advice (team of experts)		.908	22.68	.702	.493
Energy Dependency Risk		.803	20.07	.607	.368
Velocity of Profit		.646	16.14	.530	.281

Table 15. Cronbach's Alpha Reliability Statistics for ERAS Instrument by Factor (*N* = 276)

Factors	Alpha, if Item Deleted	α
I. Customer and Resources		.6691
Q16. Owner Time Dependency	.6259	
Q24. Customer Activity/Turnover	.5925	
Q25. Customer Credit Risk	.6203	
Q26. Line of Credit	.6056	
Q27. Market Potential	.6443	
II. Security		.6115
Q32. Social Responsibility	.5802	
Q33. Environment/Weather	.5807	
Q34. Security/Crime Vulnerability	.4889	
Q35. Terrorism/Vulnerability	.5046	
III. Operations		.6381
Q17. Labor Intensity	.6581	
Q18. Overhead Costs	.4562	
Q19. Equipment Investment	.4927	
IV. External Pressures		.5253
Q20. Internet/Technology	.4802	
Q28. Barriers to Entry	.3528	
Q31. Government Regulation	.4316	
V. Other and Alternate Factors		.5436*
Q21. Experts for Advice	.3529	
Q22. Intellectual Capital/Property	.3817	
Q23. Velocity of Profit	.4785	
Q36. Energy Dependency Risk	.3914	

*Note. Q29-competition intensity, Q-30 economic risk and Q37-globalization risk were deleted from factor scores for establishing criterion validity and increasing Cronbach's Alpha coefficients for each factor.

    Field (2005) argued Cronbach's Alpha should not be used to measure unidimensionality. In terms of a measuring (α) in a factor analysis, individual factors were measured separately. Since this study uses a factor analysis methodology and ERAS is a 37-item instrument (based on the number of items), a minimum benchmark set for the Cronbach's Alpha is .5 or higher. This indicates the Cronbach's Alpha coefficients for ERAS met and surpassed the minimum standard for the benchmark coefficient of .5 or higher. Thus, ERAS is considered a moderately reliable instrument. Because it did not reach the benchmark of alpha greater than .7, the calculated factors scores rather than the simple sums were used to assess criterion validity.

Factor structure of the ERAS instrument. As a result, both the principal axis factoring (PAF) and principal component analysis (PCA) resulted in five factors (see Table 16 and Figure 3) with 19 items. The new emerging factors were identified as (a) customer and resources, (b) security, (c) operations, (d) external pressures, and (e) other/alternate factors.

Table 16. Factor Structure of ERAS Instrument and Defining Variables

Factors	Defining Variables
1. Customer and Resources	Q16. owner time dependency Q24. customer activity/turnover Q25. customer credit risk Q26. line of credit Q27. market potential
2. Security	Q32. social responsibility/ entrepreneurship Q33. environment/weather Q34. security/crime vulnerability Q35. terrorism/vulnerability
3. Operations	Q17. labor intensity Q18. overhead costs Q19. equipment and systems investment
4. External Pressures	Q20. internet/technology Q28. barriers to entry constraints Q31. government regulations constraints
5. Other and Alternate Factors	Q21. experts (team of experts for advice) Q22. intellectual property risk Q23. velocity of profit risk Q36. energy dependency risk

Note. Items Q29-competition intensity, Q-30 economic risk and Q37-globalization risk were deleted from the final structure.

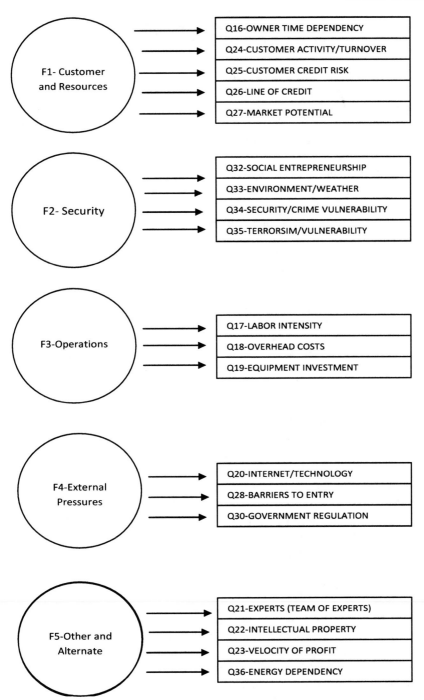

Figure 3. ERAS conclusive factor structure

Factor scores of nascent and incumbent SMEs. The results of the ERAS item responses of the means and standard deviation are illustrated in Table 17. To compute the factor scores, the researcher used the *Sum Scores–Standardized Variables* approach. This method uses scale raw scores to the same mean and standard deviation before summing. The advantages of using this approach are: (a) useful to deal with observed variables that vary widely in terms of standard deviation; and (b) refinement worth effort unless observed variables are reasonably similar in the size of standard deviations. The only consideration is if the standard deviations of raw scores are similar, sum scores without standardizing are easier to compute (DiStefano, Zhu, & Mîndrilă, 2009). A T-test was used to compare the cumulative factor scores between nascent and incumbent SMEs.

There were differences between nascent and incumbent in terms of means and standard deviations of total responses. The total factor score were as follows: nascent SMEs ($M = 58.60$, $SD = 26.6$); and incumbent SMEs ($M = 66.75$, $SD = 26.1$). Logistic regression factor scores were generated by SPSS as a result of the factor analysis. These were used to assess how well ERAS predicted entrepreneurial risk orientation (ERO) behavior between nascent and incumbent SMEs (see Table 17).

Criterion validity. For criterion validity to be established, the central Measurement issue to be addressed is *prediction*. It is defined as the degree to which the instrument predicts a well-accepted indicator of a given concept (Bryant, 2000). To assess criterion validity, a logistic regression was performed to predict nascent and incumbent SMEs evaluating the predictive capability of ERAS instrument.

The purpose of logistic regression, the value that is being predicted represents a probability; it is used as a categorical predictor variable (Ayres, 2007; Harman, 1976; Field, 2005; George & Mallery, 2003; Kachigan, 1991). Logistical regression is a kind of regression analysis that is used when the dependent variable is dichotomous (two-item response); it is used to predict whether something either will occur or not. The criterion variable is categorical and the predictor variable usually included, both categorical and continuous variables. This allows the researcher to estimate the probability of an event occurring based on the values for the predictor variables (Field, 2005; Green, Salkind, & Akey, 2000; Nicol & Pexman, 2007; Tabachnick & Fidell, 2007; Vogt, 1993).

A logistic regression analysis was performed on the ERAS instrument for this research study. The independent variables included the regression factor scores for the identified factors of risk illustrated in Table 18. The coefficients indicate there were two different predictive indicators of ERO behavior: (a) customer and resources factors, and (b) operations factors. The analysis was performed using SPSS 17.0. A test of the full model with all predictors against a constant-only model was statistically significant, X^2 ($N = 276$) SE $= .185$, $p < .001$).

Table 17. Factor Scores, Means, and Standard Deviations of Nascent and Incumbent SMEs (N = 276)

Factors and Items	Nascent (n = 193)		Incumbent (n = 83)	
	M	SD	M	SD
I. Customer and Resources				
16. Owner Time Depend.	2.64	1.462	3.39	1.404
24. Customer Activity/Turn.	3.28	1.228	3.92	1.084
25. Customer Credit Risk	2.27	1.212	2.98	1.316
26. Line of Credit	2.51	1.287	3.19	1.410
27. Market Potential	3.93	1.394	4.67	0.665
Total	14.63	6.583	18.15	5.879
II. Security				
32. Social Entrepreneurship	1.77	1.181	1.65	1.184
33. Environment/Weather	2.78	1.416	2.82	1.398
34. Security/Crime Vulnerability	2.58	1.340	2.87	1.496
35. Terrorism/Vulnerability	2.96	1.338	2.88	1.517
Total	10.09	5.275	10.22	5.595
III. Operations				
17. Labor Intensity	3.31	1.260	3.59	1.307
18. Overhead Costs	2.74	1.130	3.29	1.245
19. Equipment Investment	3.08	1.359	3.49	1.329
Total	9.13	3.749	10.37	3.881
IV. External Pressures				
20. Internet /Technology	3.21	1.320	3.49	1.282
28. Barriers to Entry	2.85	1.340	3.17	1.395
31. Government Regulation	3.19	1.418	3.55	1.382
Total	9.25	4.078	10.21	4.059
V. Other and Alternate Factors				
21. Experts (Team of Experts)	2.92	1.443	3.37	1.471
22. Intellectual Property Risk	2.77	1.660	2.86	1.540
23. Velocity of Profit Risk	3.45	1.235	4.23	0.992
36. Energy Dependency Risk	3.18	1.319	3.67	1.371
Total	12.32	5.657	14.13	5.374
Overall Total	58.60	26.66	66.75	26.16

Note. The means and standard deviations are computed as an average of the items within the subclass scale. This is inclusive of both nascent and incumbent SMEs.

Table 18 shows the regression coefficients, Wald statistics, and the significances of the five predictors. Beta (β) indicates the effect of the *predictor variable* on the *predicted variable* (George & Mallery, 2003; Glenberg, 1996; Tabachnick & Fidell, 2008). The coefficients in Table 18 indicate that two of the factor variables were significant predictors of ERO. The predictor statistics were as follows: Customer and Resources (β = 1.030, $p < .000$); and operations (β = .416, $p < .007$). Logistic regression increased predictability from 69.8% to 73.1% with the FACTOR 1 - Customer and Resources (*p*) coefficient scores and FACTOR 3 - Operations (*p*) coefficient scores as the best predictors of nascent and incumbent status. Thus, ERAS appears to be a moderate predictor of ERO between nascent and incumbent SMEs.

Table 18. Results of Logistic Regression Analysis Predicting ERO Behavior Using Nascent vs. Incumbent Classification as A Dependent Variable ($N = 276$)

Predictor Variables	β	SE	Wald	df	p	Exp(B)
Customer and Resources	**1.030**	**.203**	**25.73**	**1.00**	**.000**	**2.801**
Security	-.245	.155	2.49	1.00	.114	.783
Operations	**.416**	**.155**	**7.20**	**1.00**	**.007**	**1.517**
External Pressures	-.106	.169	.389	1.00	.533	.900
Other/ Alternate Factors	-.039	.162	.058	1.00	.809	.962

Note. *Nascent vs. incumbent are the dependent variables.
Factor scores are the independent variables

Comparing the ERAS theoretical model with conclusive factor structure. The results of the findings are presented in a comparison between the ERAS theoretical model and the results of the conclusive factor structure from the factor analysis. The results of the factor loadings are presented in five factors (see Table 19). The first column addresses the ERAS theoretical model proposed loadings. The second column presents the results of the factor loadings from the formal study. Notably, there is a significant difference, in terms of structure, as evidenced in the conclusive factor analyses (both PAF and PCA). The factor structure was significantly different from the theoretical model. This was most evident in factors three and four.

The results of the factor analysis of the 22 items did not concur with the ERAS theoretical model. There are two main issues, to consider, in examining the comparison between the theoretical model and factor loading findings. First, there is some structural agreement between the two. Second, the conclusive factor analysis structure confirms the appropriate factor loadings. Therefore, the ERAS theoretical model does not completely explain the factor structure of results from the data set (see Table 19).

The rationale for why so many items were removed from the conclusive factor structure was because those items had factor coefficient loadings below .3. Secondly, non-Likert items were removed (e.g., 2-item binary scale, 5-item multiple-choice scales, 6-item multiple-choice scales, and 11-item multiple-choice scales) because they could not load within a 5-factor solution. Lastly, other non-Likert items such as continuous variables were removed because they could not load within a 5-factor solution.

Table 19. Comparison between the ERAS Theoretical Model and Conclusive Factor Structure

ERAS Theoretical Model	Conclusive Factor Structure
1. Personal Characteristics Risk	1. Customer and Resources
Q1-Gender (a)	Q16-Owner Time Dependency
Q5-Ethnicity (a)	Q24-Customer Activity/Turn.
Q6-Education Level (a)	Q25-Customer Credit Risk
Q7-Compensation (a)	Q26-Line of Credit
Q9-Length of Business Ownership (a)	Q27-Market Potential
Q10-Expertise in Industry (a)	
2. Intangible Operations Risk	2. Security
Q14-Business Entity Type	Q32-Social Responsibility Risk
Q15-Capital Investment	Q33-Environment/ Weather
Q16-Time Intensity	Q34-Security/Crime Vuln.
	Q35-Terrorism/ Vulnerability

ERAS Theoretical Model	Conclusive Factor Structure
3. Enterprise Operations Risk	3. Operations
Q17-Business Entity Type	Q17-Labor Intensity
Q18-Overhead Costs	Q18-Overhead Costs
Q19-Equipment Investment	Q19-Equipment Investment
Q20-Internet /Technology	
Q21-Experts for Advice	
Q22-Intellectual Capital/ Property	
Q23-Velocity of Profit	
Q24-Customer Activity/ Turnover	
4. Market Climate Risks	4. External Pressures
*Q25-Customer Credit Risk	Q20-Internet /Technology
*Q26-Line of Credit	Q28-Barriers to Entry
Q27-Market Potential	Q31-Government Regulation
Q28-Barriers to Entry	
Q29-Competition Intensity	
Q30-Economic Risk	
Q31-Government Regulation	
Q32-Social Responsibility Risk	
5. Business Environment Risks	5. Other and Alternate Factors
Q33-Environment/Weather	Q21-Experts for Advice
Q34-Security/Crime Vuln.	Q22-Intellectual Capital/Prop.
Q35-Terrorism/Vulnerability	Q23-Velocity of Profit
Q36-Energy Dependency Risk	Q36-Energy Dependency Risk
Q37-Globalization Risk	

Note. *Items with asterisk were not in the original ERAS theoretical model. (a) Indicates personal factors were not included in the conclusive factor analysis.

Summary of Chapter 4

This chapter presented the results of the data derived from the sample population of small-to-medium business enterprises (SMEs). The major characteristics of the samples were described. The chapter further discusses data sources, measurement, and statistical analysis.

The demographic descriptive statistics of SME owners and participant descriptive statistics were discussed. Subsequently, validity of ERAS was assessed using Bryant's (2000) model to assess the validity of ERAS. Factors items were omitted from the factor structure due to: low factor coefficients loadings; and failure to meet the minimum factor coefficient benchmark of .3. Construct validity was supported using a principal axis factoring (PAF) to identify five factors among the Likert items. Under this face validity, convergent validity and discriminant validity were established. For establishing content validity, a principal component analysis (PCA) was conducted. Content validity was also established from the literature review, Cronbach alphas, subject matter expert panels, and findings from the pilot test. Criterion validity was assessed using factor scores in a logistic regression to assess ability to distinguish between nascent and incumbent SMEs. ERAS was confirmed as holding both construct and content validity. In assessment of criterion validity, two of the five factors were good predictors of nascent and incumbent SMEs.

Chapter Five will present a discussion of the results of the data analysis and the conclusions drawn from the findings. The next chapter will also present the limitations of the study; and the future potential directions for possible research.

Discussion and Conclusions

Introduction

The primary objective of this study was to develop and validate an instrument to assess entrepreneurial risk. This was accomplished through an exhaustive review of the literature, and the subsequent development of a theoretical model and instrument. The ERAS instrument is a first-generation instrument developed to assess entrepreneurial risk behavior of SMEs. It was conceptually developed using all the risk factors that could possibly have a direct influence on the failure or success of an enterprise. ERAS could possibly be a vital instrument in the fields of entrepreneurship and small business. Instrument validity is an important concept for a first-generation instrument.

The ERAS Theoretical Model is based on the following five factors of entrepreneurial risk (a) personal characteristics, (b) intangible operations, (c) enterprise operations, (d) market climate, and (e) business environment. As a result of the theoretical model development, the ERAS instrument was created. ERAS is a 37-item scale. Data was collected using ERAS from a population sample of 276 small-to-medium business enterprises (SME). The ERAS instrument was pilot-tested for screening item errors and question adjustments. The data collected using ERAS was analyzed to determine instrument validity and reliability; and to assess the results of the collected data. The goal of the research was to establish three types of validity: construct, content and criterion.

In this study, the researcher attempted to fill a gap in the literature by focusing on the risk behavior of enterprises, rather than the risk behavior of entrepreneurs. The researcher investigated what types of risk factors tended represent significant contributing factors to the success or failure of an enterprise. Next, the researcher attempted to analyze the major determinants of risks among the factors. Lastly, the researcher attempted to investigate the effects of the risk factors on firm behavior. The research study was guided by the following research question(s):

1. Does the Entrepreneurial Risk Assessment Scale (ERAS) provide evidence of adequate instrument validity?
2. Does ERAS provide evidence of adequate instrument reliability?

Relating the Results of the Findings to the Literature

There were two notable observations relating the study findings to the literature. The literature review established the original dimensions for the ERAS instrument. The first observation was concerned with the predictor variables of entrepreneurial risk orientation (ERO). The findings indicated there were two different predictive indicators ERO behavior with SMEs: (a) customer and resources factors, and (b) operations factors. Notably, nothing in the literature concurred or supported these findings. Although, the original factor items were not retained as a component, nothing in the predictor factors was supported in the literature review. However, this did provide an interesting statistical result and did establish this as a basis for item development and possible further research. As observed by the researcher, this is because the predictor variables in the study may have not captured all the possible predictor variables. In addition, although the researcher's findings on the two predictors of risk factors were observed, they could not be compared directly with any of the any previous findings in the literature.

The second observation was the issues of gender, ethnicity, and education level. The literature indicated that gender, ethnicity, and education level were contributing factors to entrepreneurial risk and the success and failure of an enterprise. The study findings did not support those conclusions. The literature review suggested gender as a risk variable was found to be a significant factor in the success or failure of an enterprise (Browne, 2001; Collins, 2007; Robb, 2002; Shane, 2008; Watson, 2003).

However, this study results stated otherwise. The researcher found weak evidence of gender having a relationship with risk factors. The results of this study are inconsistent with the findings of Robb (2002) and Shane (2008) concerning the influence of gender and ethnicity on entrepreneurial risk and possible failure. Unlike Shane (2008), who relied on a significant amount of secondary data for evidence of firm survival due to gender and ethnicity, the current study found no statistical evidence that supported those variables as predictors of entrepreneurial risk or predictors of failure. As observed by the researcher, the logistic regression findings do not support gender as one of the predictor variables in the study; there did not appear to be any consistent differences between both genders in the data. Also, the logistic regression results did not support ethnicity as predictor variable of entrepreneurial risk.

The results of this study are consistent with the findings of Collins (2007) concerning the influence of education. Collins found that education did not impact entrepreneurial success in terms of gender. The study's findings also did not support education level as a predictor variable in terms of entrepreneurial risk. Overall, this study found no evidence that supports gender, ethnicity, and education level as significant predictors of entrepreneurial risk or possible impact on failure.

Conclusions from the Research
Since the previous literature left many questions unanswered, the researcher attempted to validate a first-generation instrument for measuring entrepreneurial risk (ER). As evident in the literature, ER is a more complex and a

critical component in the failure or success of an enterprise. However, this research also suggests that entrepreneurial risk is not based on gender, ethnicity, or education level. Numerous determinants of entrepreneurial risk have been identified in the literature (e.g., industry experience, market saturation, customer turnover, economic factors). The current research provides support for the literature, suggesting there are numerous risk factors that influence enterprise success or failure. The research also suggests there is a need to examine SMEs in many dimensions and enterprise dynamics to assess their risk orientation.

This study has been one of the few entrepreneurship studies to specifically focus on enterprise risk and support it with empirical results. These findings provide a beginning for evaluating entrepreneurial risk on specific risk variables. For example, it would be beneficial to investigate the risk factors in a capacity of financial services environment with a focus on lending decision-making. Despite the research, the instrument is still in its infancy in terms of validity and reliability. There are still population groups in locations that could not be addressed during the time in which this research was conducted. In the opinion of the researcher, ERAS could provide an opportunity to gather data on risk from those other populations and most definitely extend beyond the geographical area represented in this study. The rationale behind this would be to determine whether similar findings could be expected from the instrument utilized in a different capacity.

While conducting the study, the researcher observed there were many emerging financial, cultural, and market trends and differences in various geographical areas domestically, as well as globally. This observation of those emerging trends could cause some SMEs to be more vulnerable to varying degrees of entrepreneurial risk. By facilitating new interest in the subject of entrepreneurial risk, this could have far-reaching effects on banks, venture capitalists, investors, and emerging entrepreneurs seeking to start a business. Considering the staggering number of new businesses that fail, understanding of ER as a concept is now more important than ever.

From this research, numerous determinants of entrepreneurial risk have been identified in the literature (e.g. inadequate industry experience, customer activity, customer turnover, inability, competition intensity, and failure to protect intellectual and proprietary property). One of the significant findings is there was an interesting mix of predictor variables that revealed there are two different predictive indicators of ERO behavior (FACTOR 1 - Customer and Resources; and FACTOR 3 – Operations). This compared differently with the other non-predictors that were had low significance coefficients (FACTOR 2 – Security, FACTOR 4 – External Pressures, and FACTOR 5 – Other and Alternate Factors).

In examination of the data, there were no conclusive research findings supporting differences between nascent and incumbent SMEs. The overall study findings suggests there are some, but not significant, differences between nascent and incumbent SMEs. The results of the data collected for this study did not support the assertion that nascent SMEs are more risky than incumbent SMEs. The standard deviations and means were not significantly different. In the researcher's opinion, the findings should be interpreted with caution. The reason is that there was not enough evidence to support that from the data. Perhaps a larger sample of 500 would have resulted in some differences. The study had a shortcoming in terms of presenting their differences. The results presented in this study on nascent and incumbent SMEs warrant further research.

Factor scores and observations. There were issues concerning factor scores with the ERAS instrument in this study. The major issue with the factor scores in this study is the problem of *indeterminancy*. Indeterminancy, in mathematics and statistics means there is an infinite number of sets of factor scores that could be computed from any given factor analysis that would be equally consistent with the same number of factor loading (Brown, 2006; Cureton & D'Agostino, 1983; Gorsuch, 1983; Grice, 2001; Williams, 1978). The property of indeterminancy has been known by mathematicians and statisticians since the late 1920s during the emergence of factor analysis. The ramifications of indeterminancy are a serious concern to validity and reliability. Because of this, an infinite number of factor scores possible, any one set can only be considered estimates of undefined theoretical scores (Gorsuch, 1983; Harman, 1976; Mulaik 1972; Rummel, 1970).

To address the issues of indeterminancy with the factor scores, the researcher utilized a simple and non-refined method to compute the factor scores. The researcher used the *Sum Scores —Standardized Variables* approach. Non-refined factor scores are thought to be more stable across samples than refined methods. This means the obtained results do not heavily depend on the particular sample used (DiStefano, Zhu, & Mîndrilă, 2009). For example, non-refined methods do not achieve a set mean and/or standard deviation for each of the factor scores. However, the mean and standard deviation of the factors will be dependent upon the characteristics of the items (e.g., scale of measurement, variability in data, etc.) (DiStefano, Zhu, & Mîndrilă, 2009).

In reviewing the factor scores, there were only slight differences between nascent and incumbent in terms of means and standard deviations of total responses. In examining all the factors' standard deviations and means, none had any significant disparities. The only logical explanation is because there was not much diversity in terms of industry types; the majority of the SMEs were in the services industry (35.5%). Thus, there may not have been that many disparities in terms of industry types with the risk factors. In addition, the question types may have prompted the survey respondents to answer questions along a particular line of thinking when they expressed their perceptions. Therefore, the differences between nascent and incumbent SMEs in the data seem to be minimal.

It is surprising that this research shows some risk factors are more likely to have a minor impact instead of others (e.g., competition, economic forces, and market potential). Although the findings on the factor scores were determined as a predictor of risk, the study's results cannot be compared with any previous studies. The reason for this warranted since ERAS is a first-generation instrument. There is a dearth of research in this subject matter concerning enterprise risk. This is evidenced by the review of literature. There is literally an overabundance of research in the risk behavior and risk personalities of entrepreneur. There are no prior studies in the literature that pursued this inquiry of interest.

Conclusions on validity and reliability. This study was able to achieve its two primary goals: to develop and test an instrument for validity; and test the instrument for reliability. This study suggests that the ERAS instrument has achieved validity and reliability. First, the findings indicate that construct validity was achieved through statistical analysis that supported the ERAS instrument. The results of the principle axis factoring and Pearson's Correlation indicate that ERAS has construct validity. In addition, this was further achieved with subject matter expert panels.

Second, the findings indicate that content validity was achieved through a principle component analysis. This indicates that ERAS has content validity. In addition, this was further achieved with subject matter expert panels.

Third, the findings indicate that criterion validity was achieved through a logistic regression. Finally, the findings indicate that Cronbach's Alpha provided good internal consistency for the instrument,
thus achieving reliability (see Table 20).

Contribution to Field of Study in Entrepreneurship
This study contributes to the field of entrepreneurship and small business literature by shedding light on the issue of entrepreneurial risk as a new taxonomy for evaluating SMEs. Compared with previous risk behavior studies of entrepreneurs, this study attempts to open a new inquiry into assessing enterprise risk.

The importance of this research is threefold. On a theoretical level, this research (a) expands the prior research scope on entrepreneurial risk behavior, by also examining enterprise risk (ER), (b) contributes to a central theory on ER that has not been fully articulated in the prior literature, and (c) makes a contribution to the theoretical understanding of ER as a construct and contribute to the emerging entrepreneurship theory on risk and enterprise behavior.

Finally, this study attempts to fill a gap that currently exists in the prior entrepreneurship studies. There appears to be a lack of a defined theory in the prior studies on entrepreneurial risk studies. There is a need for a study on entrepreneurial risk that extends beyond examining the risk-taking personality traits and behavioral heuristics of the entrepreneur. This study is

Table 20. Summary of Measures Used for Establishing Validity and Reliability

Validity and Reliability	Measure Used	Achieved Validity/ Reliability?
Construct Validity		
Convergent Validity	Subject Matter Expert Panels	YES
Discriminant Validity	Pearson's Correlation	*NO
Face Validity	Principal Axis Factoring	YES (with PAF-1 and PAF-2)
Content Validity		
Factorial Validity or Structural Validity	Review of the Literature	YES
	Subject Matter Expert Panels	YES
	Principal Component Analysis	YES
Criterion Validity	Logistic Regression	YES (marginal - 2 predictors)
Factor Scores	T-test	YES (marginal)
Reliability	Cronbach's Alpha	YES

*Note. The Pearson's Correlation results indicate the factor coefficients are low because they are measuring dissimilar variables within each factor and not the same variables. Factor scores had issues with indeterminacy.

significant, because it can possibly contribute the establishment of a universal lexicon and taxonomy on ER in the field of entrepreneurship research.

Theoretical contributions of the study. There were four positive theoretical contributions of the study to the existing body of knowledge. The first contribution was the careful construction and development of the risk variables researched. Entrepreneurial risk behavior in enterprises is very complex and had many components. Due to the complexity of the constructs, only a limited number of factors of risk could be reasonably measured for this study. The researcher found that some factor items identified in the study could not be measured (e.g., inventory turnover, profit margin, return-on-investment and others) in the limited amount of time allocated. The decision of the researcher was to choose the five most essential measurable risk factors (e.g., competition intensity, market forces, business environment, industry experience, and others) for this study. Nevertheless, the five most critical risk factors were investigated. The use of this assessment, concerning entrepreneurial risk, was sufficient to make an investigation concerning SME's behavior (Ahwireng-Obeng & Mokgohlwa, 2002; Dollinger 1999; Hirschey, 2006; Hirschey & Pappas, 1992).

The second study contribution was the mixture of both endogenous and exogenous variables. Both variable types were a critical influence to SMEs. In the opinion of the researcher, having the presence of both variable types gives the study an advantage of examining them independently, separately and/or interdependently. This also provides an additional benefit of building SME risk behavioral profiles based on the both variable types' characteristics for further research use. The study encompasses some endogenous variables, such as operations, labor costs, and overhead costs for investigation. Additionally, the study incorporated some exogenous variables, such as customer turnover, competitor number, market forces, and weather/climatic influences (Dollinger, 1999; Everett & Watson, 1998; Hirschey, 2006; Hirschey & Pappas, 1992).

The third study contribution was the investigation of industry types. A key issue established from the literature review was that some industry types are quite diverse and may not be the best for startups. The researcher found that industry types were both a key in the development of the theoretical model and risk factors. For example, SMEs in manufacturing industries will exhibit different risk factors than SMEs in services industries. Without the industry type classifications in the ERAS instrument, the opportunity to build on this data would have been lost. Consequently, as the researcher observed some industries were not the best for startup ventures. Certain factors may influence success or failure (e.g., overhead costs, customer turnover, competition intensity, economic climate) more than others. The study examined if there were any industry characteristics that influenced the propensity of risk with SMEs (Abdelsamad & Kindling, 1978; Gaskill, Van Auken, & Manning, 1993; Ricketts, Gaskill, Van Auken & Manning, 1993; Menefee & Parnell, 2007; Porter, 1998; Strotmann, 2007). This is a key positive contribution of this study.

The final positive study contribution was the empirical examination of gender, ethnicity, and education level as risk variables on SMEs. The study provided an investigation into to the possible influence of the gender, ethnicity, and level of education variables. As the study developed, the researcher developed comprehensive statistical measures (e.g., logistic regression, T-tests and factor scores) for examining gender differences with risk factors. However, there did not appear to be any consistent risk factor differences not only with gender, but also with the variables ethnicity and education level.

In the opinion of the researcher, this gave the study a strong contribution. Interestingly, the findings of this study conflicted with the previous research findings that suggested gender and ethnicity were contributing factors to the success or failure of an enterprise (Browne, 2001; Collins, 2007; Robb, 2002; Shane, 2008). In summary, by exploring entrepreneurial risk, this empirical evidence attempted to establish an important link among critical studies in the entrepreneurship literature in terms of the five factors discussed in this study. Accordingly, future research should be directed toward examining the relationship between enterprise risk and enterprise failure.

Limitations of the Research

Self-reported data. A key limitation was the use of self-reported data. Data reflected the owner's perception of risk, which may have been distorted or incomplete. Some of the participants may not have properly comprehend the subject matter of some of the survey questions or been selective on answering questions. For example, responses to questions concerning salary or compensation from the business were a challenge. Many participants did not answer the question. Based on the results from the factor analyses, the researcher would suggest further scrutiny of the non-responses to survey questions. This would minimize some of the issues with the use of self-reported data. In the researcher's opinion, the reason for the non-answers was due to the fact the question was a continuous variable. Fowler (1995) argued that with survey research questions concerning salary or income, respondents prefer questions in a Likert-type style that provide a range. Since, some of questions had continuous variables (e.g., compensation, age, and capital invested); it was a factor as to why they were not answered. The researcher approached this shortcoming of the self-reported data with caution. This was a limitation to the study.

Industry types. A second limitation was the lack of diversity in the types of industries assessed. There were very few manufacturing, wholesale, and retail trade firms. Possibly, there might have been different results if there had been more diversity of industry types. The opinion of the researcher is that the study relied too heavily on SMEs in the services industry. For example, there could have been more retail and wholesale trade firms for the study. There also may have been more SMEs in the agricultural industry. The major limitation of this study is that some industries were underrepresented in the sample size. This is a positive start for gathering vital data on industries, however not having more industries represented will only tell some of the story; the whole story needs to be told. A majority of the limitation with industries was attributed to demographic, market sector and geographic influences.

Ethnic composition. A third limitation concerned the ethnic diversity of study participants. This lack of diversity, in both the local sector and geographic location, may have influenced the results. For example, a statewide sample of respondents would have resulted in stronger and more diverse ethnic composition. Another example, the limited access to particular ethnic groups was a constraint. It would have been an improvement to the ethnic composition of the sample if the researcher could have had better access to other sub-groups through other chambers of commerce. This would have provided for a richer sample ethnicity wise, but also would have provided some interesting data and a platform for further research. The study was limited to the sample population of the city. The geographical constraints and lack of population diversity is indicative of the sample taken from this population. Further research is needed to investigate findings with a more ethnically and socioeconomically diverse sample.

Geographical constraints. The last limitation was concerned with the study's geographic limitations. The research was limited to the San Antonio area (Bexar County). For example, similar to the limitations with the ethnic composition, the geographic location may have influenced the study's results. Additionally, the generalizability of this study is limited to the San Antonio (Bexar County) area's population was a constraint. The data were collected from only one city population. The geographical limitation was a contributing influence to this study's population sample, industry types, and economic factors. While the ERAS scale factor coefficient loadings are encouraging in this sample, further studies are needed to address SME differences beyond the geographical constraints.

Time constraints. The window of opportunity to collect the data was very limited (less than a semester). It would have been more beneficial to take more time to collect additional surveys. For example, the researcher would have preferred to achieve a survey number of 400 to 1,000. A larger sample with more varied business industries and SMEs would have served to clarify the findings of the current study further. This would have allowed the researcher to eliminate the surveys that were not useful to the study. Due to this constraint, there was not enough time to collect more data.

Time and research costs. Another example was the issue of cost and time of conducting this study. It was another constraint with time. The researcher had a abundant amount of available time to conduct the research. However, the cost of conducting more research at the expense of time was a constraint. There was no feasible way to collect more data in the time horizon allotted for this study because of cost. The more time exerted to collect data, the more costs were being incurred. It was not cost-prohibitive to spend more time to collect more data. Had the two issues been rectified, more data could have been collected and more funding could have been available. If more data were collected data, this would have possibly provided some interesting results.

Recommendations for Future Research

The purpose of this study was to develop and validate an instrument. Developing a new instrument can be problematic. In developing a first generation-instrument, there are challenges for a researcher beyond data collection. The rigor of developing and validating an instrument is taxing and consuming. Based on the research findings, there are suggestions for further research. Since the Entrepreneurial Risk Assessment Scale (ERAS) instrument was developed specifically for this study, it is the first of its kind. There are many opportunities for developing a better ERAS instrument. The potential for ERAS is enormous. With further refinements, ERAS may be helpful in assessing the risk of small-to-medium business enterprises (SME). For example, refinements such as a redesign to make the instrument easier to administer and collect data would be a good step in further development. Further development will be the key in reaching that goal. Subsequent panels of subject matter experts will be needed to improve the assessment capabilities of ERAS. The primary value of ERAS is its potential capability to examine the business risk of an enterprise. Based on the findings in this study, there are suggestions offered for further research.

The factor items were reduced from 22 to 19 items within five factors. The three factor items that were eliminated were Q29-Competition, Q30-Economic risk, and Q37-Globalization. The factor items were removed the factor coefficients fell below the .3 benchmark established for this study. The results of the principle component analysis (PCA) study suggest that factor loadings differed significantly with the theoretical model. Overall, both PAF and PCA achieved factorial validity and reliability.

The implications of eliminating these three items require further investigation. For example, it would be useful to determine how applicable the ERAS instrument would be for market sectors such as tourism or seasonal businesses. It would be interesting to examine those industries and compare their factors and predictor variables. Competition, economic and globalization are essential variables. For future research, maybe using another instrument or significantly modifying the ERAS instrument will address the issues with the three variables. These factors will be re-introduced in the ERAS instrument for future research with larger, more diverse sample.

Research endogenous and exogenous variables as factors. A first recommendation would be to conduct another factor analysis of this data, by examining endogenous and exogenous as two factors with SMEs. Research examining those distinct variables in the ERAS instrument could provide some significant insight. A study specifically designed to examine risk behavior of endogenous and exogenous factors is an excellent opportunity. For example, it would be interesting to conduct a logistic regression on both variables to see if there are any differences in significance (p). Another example would be to compute a T-test on both variables; this would possibly provide some useful information. This would extend the scope of this study and provide a valuable contribution to the field of study in entrepreneurship.

Longitudinal study. The second recommendation would be to conduct a longitudinal study on risk and business failure with SMEs. Further predictive ability could be achieved by returning to these same businesses five years from now and see if ERAS accurately predicted survival or failure. An example of this would be to form a strategic alliance with the Small Business Administration (SBA). To conduct a longitudinal study, the researcher would track SME borrowers annually until the business fails or discontinues. Then compare the risk variables at the time of loan with the data during the life of the business. This study would have an objective of further examining the risk and failure correlation based on key variables in ERAS such as age, gender, ethnicity, education-level, industry type, competition intensity, business experience, capital intensity and most notably market forces. This would thereby provide more insights into enterprise risk orientation as it correlates to business enterprise failure.

Apply study on a state and national basis. A third recommendation is to conduct a similar study in other geographic locations within the United States. To extend the research to other geographic locations within the state and the U.S. could further validate the instrument and perhaps provide additional information on the effect of risk factors. Some risk factors may be more acclimated to different conditions in geographic regions. Under different geographic conditions, SME may respond differently to risk factors in the ERAS instrument. The findings from additional research on national basis could further the development of ERAS as a measurement instrument.

Apply study on an international basis. A fourth recommendation would be to apply the ERAS instrument to the international sector for validation of the instrument. This study focused minimally on globalization as a risk variable. To extend the study, outside the United States, to examine the impact of risk forces would be interesting. Different cultures and different SMEs may respond to the risk factors in the ERAS instrument differently. Notably, the influence of key international factors such as cultural differences, cultural forces, political forces, governmental forces, economic forces and others could be enlightening. Application of ERAS in an international capacity could potentially underscore differences and focus on other risk factors not prevalent in domestic SMEs. For example, entry into global markets creates new opportunities for exports, but there is the problem of firms' vulnerability to foreign tariffs and import restrictions (Hull, 2005). There are five general categories of globalization risk that can be further researched for a future study. These categories are: (a) cultural risk, (b) currency risk, (c) government policy risk, (d) expropriation risk, and (e) transnational competition risk (Ball et al., 2006; Hirschey, 2006). However, further research and development are necessary. The research potential of applying ERAS in an international capacity would be interesting.

Development of new factors. A fifth recommendation for further research would be the development of a possible sixth factor, technological risk forces. The opportunity to continue and develop the ERAS theoretical model is tremendous. A first step would be to adding technology as a construct. Since technology and information technology are driving forces in many industries, it would be essential to measure them. Technology continues to be a consequential factor in the success or failure of an enterprise. The influence of technology on the success or failure of a firm is critical. In the opinion of the researcher, to establish technology as a risk factor it will involve research of the literature. The research will be much similar to the development of the other factors. For example, because technology means different things to different industries, a set of variables to measure it as a construct has to be established. It will be challenge. Can you measure technology as a risk factor and compare technology-driven firms with non-technology driven firms? That question needs to be answered. The determinants of developing technology as a risk factor will need to be carefully examined. The opportunity to continue to build upon this instrument and theoretical model for future research is promising. As an individual construct, technological risk needs to be further developed in a factor analysis.

Research behavior of franchises vs. non-franchises. The sixth recommendation is to conduct a research study that would examine the risk behavior of franchises and non-franchises. Researchers have the opportunity to examine franchises vs. non-franchises further. As evidenced in the literature, franchises do fail and further examining their idiosyncrasies compared to non-franchises is an opportunity. In the opinion of the researcher, it would behoove an investigator to expand on this as a research opportunity. While this study was not able to examine the differences between the two extensively, there is an opportunity to investigate further. The objective would be to determine if there are risk factors that are endemic to one group versus the other group.

Expand the instrument for examining web-based SMEs. The seventh recommendation is to expand the instrument to include Internet-based businesses. At present, the instrument is targeted toward assessing risk with traditional brick and mortar-type businesses. The reason for this would be to analyze web-based SMEs by developing a new instrument and comparing the results with the prior research on traditional SMEs. The purpose of this is to build on the research conducted on traditional businesses. As Internet firms are developing, an instrument that can assess their risk levels could be instrumental in evaluating their potential. An instrument with different risk factors that are unique to Web-based enterprises may need to be developed to assess their risk properties. Further expanding to a more varied sample, the ERAS instrument would decrease the chances of sampling bias.

Further develop a mixed method instrument design. The eighth recommendation would be to conduct a study utilizing a mixed quantitative-qualitative study design. In the opinion of the researcher, a strong recommendation would be to modify the ERAS instrument to make it more inclusive of dual research designs (quantitative and qualitative). For example, a mixed-method would provide the advantage of *complementarity*, which the results from one research method supports and reinforces the use of another method (Caracelli & Greene, 1997). Integrating a qualitative component would both *confirm* and *support* the quantitative findings of the ERAS instrument and provide a holistic perspective to the findings. By implementing a qualitative component this could formulate a specialized instrument that has the capability investigate business risk behavior in more depth. Although the finalized version of the ERAS asked some open-ended survey questions (e.g. age, years of business experience, and capital investment amount), there are opportunities to exploit the qualitative characteristics of the instrument further.

Apply to academic research on entrepreneurship. A final recommendation would be to apply the research on entrepreneurship in an academic environment. As mentioned earlier, further academic research on SMEs would provide fertile ground for exploring new concepts in entrepreneurship. One such research possibility would be to examine those variables that did not have significant factor loadings (economic risk, competition intensity, and globalization risk) further. There is a possibility of using those variables separately in another factor analysis, comparable to the analyses in this study. The objective would be to determine if the loadings with those factors would lead to more in-depth findings on the entrepreneurial risk behavior in firms.

Develop a more defined taxonomy on SMEs. The research could be used by extending the literature to build a more defined taxonomy on SMEs. Further developing SME classifications such as micro-enterprises, franchises, non-franchises, nascent and incumbent would be interesting. By exploring different classifications of SME identification, ERAS could be used as a classification tool and further distinguish those SMEs by their risk behavior. Perhaps by focusing on employee size as a benchmark, this could produce some interesting findings. ERAS could also be used to build the theory if SME class identification were included to see how they affected other risk variables in the instrument.

Implications for Practice and Future Uses of ERAS Instrument

Governmental agencies that counsel businesses. Further evaluation of the business risk or entrepreneurial risk behavior would be useful for assisting the Small Business Administration (SBA) and Small Business Development Centers (SBDC). The research on a SMEs and risk factors would be useful in assisting in the evaluation of lending decisions and counseling to SMEs. This would provide an interesting approach in the use of ERAS, once thoroughly validated, as an evaluation tool for governmental agencies.

Practitioners in the field. Another possibility for practice and use would be for practitioners in the fields (bankers, venture capitalist, financial institutions, etc.) that study and research businesses. ERAS would provide the practitioners in the field an assessment tool. While ERAS has some structural similarities to Kaplan and Norton's (1996) "Balanced Scorecard," it can provide a different assessment capability. Perhaps ERAS could be utilized as an additional assessment tool in the arsenal of assessment tools. ERAS could also provide a more suitable assessment focusing on specific risk factors that are critical to counseling SMEs and examining business risk.

Business schools. ERAS could be very useful in business schools. It could be most useful in university entrepreneurship courses. Since entrepreneurship is still an emerging field of study, this would provide an excellent opportunity to use ERAS as a teaching tool. There are many ways ERAS could be used as an instruction tool to illustrate entrepreneurial risk principles and startup dynamics. Scholars could use ERAS as teaching and research tools to further explore entrepreneurial risk and business risk.

Summary of Chapter 5

This chapter presented a discussion of the implications from the results of the data analysis. Content and construct validity were established. To test for criterion validity, ERAS was used to distinguish between nascent and incumbent SMEs. The two (exogenous) factors (a) customer and resources, and (c) operations were significant predictors. A return in several years to see which of the sample businesses have survived would further establish criterion validity.

The second section focused on the limitations of the study. The limitations of the study were not a significant factor in the results. The third section focused on the contributions of the study to the field of entrepreneurship. The fourth section focused on the conclusions of the research.

The fifth section focused on recommendations for future research. Those recommendations for future research were: (a) expand the instrument, (b) include Internet-based/technological firms, (c) expand study to a national and global platform, (d) perfect the instrument, and (e) employ additional statistical analyses for examining other characteristics of the data. The last section discussed the implications of the study.

The theoretical model presented in this research is a small part of the puzzle. Very few empirical studies have specifically examined the enterprise risk behavior of SMEs. The problem of business failure was a driving impetus for this study. A large part of building the theoretical model for this research is curiosity of business risk. The adage, "all businesses are guilty until proven innocent" was more plausible than first realized when this study was untaken as a dissertation. The risks involved with starting and maintaining a business enterprise are considerable. The major problems with the pursuit of entrepreneurship are the significant forces of risk that are involved. While the results of this study did not confirm or deny the statement, the results of this study did provide evidence that the factors (a) customer and resources, and (c) operations were reliable predictors of risk behavior. Thus, the findings prove that SMEs have risks that cause them to be "guilty until proven innocent."

References

Aaker, D. & Day, G. (1990). *Marketing research* (4th ed.). New York, NY: John Wiley & Sons

Abdelsamad, M. H. & Kindling, A. (1978). Why small businesses fail. *Advanced Management Journal, 43*(2), 24-40. Retrieved from http://proquest. umi.com/pqdweb?did=7580072&sid=1&Fmt=2&clientId=1354&RQT =309&VName=PQD

Acito, F. & Anderson, R. (1986). A simulation study of factor score indeterminacy. *Journal of Marketing Research, 23*(1), 111-118.

Acs, Z. (1992). Small business economics: A global perspective. *Challenge, 35*(6), 38. Retrieved from http://proquest.umi.com/pqdweb?did= 273754&sid=9&Fmt=2&clientId=1354&RQT=309&VName=PQD

Afifi, A. & Clark, V. (1984). *Computer-aided multivariate analysis.* Belmont, CA: Lifetime Learning Publications.

Ahwireng-Obeng, F. & Mokgohlwa, J.P. (2002). Entrepreneurial risk allocation in public-private infrastructure provision in South Africa, *South African Journal of Business Management, 33*(4), 27-39.

Allen, J. & Yen, W. (1979). *Introduction to measurement theory.* Belmont, CA: Wadsworth.

Aloulou, W., & Fayolle, A. (2005, March). A conceptual approach of entrepreneurial orientation within small business context. *Journal of Enterprising Culture, 13*(1), 24-45. Retrieved from http://search.ebscohost.com/ login.aspx?direct=true&db=bth&AN=17587113&site=bsi-live&scope=site

Altma, E. (1968). Financial ratios, discriminant analysis, and the prediction of corporate bankruptcy, *Journal of Financial 22*, 589-609.

Anderson, D., Sweeny, D. & Williams, T. (1990). *Statistics for business and economics* (5th ed.). St. Paul, MN: West Publishing.

Amit, R., Glosten, L., & Muller, E. (1993). Challenges to theory development in entrepreneurship research. *Journal of Management Studies, 30*(5), 815-834. Retrieved from http://search.ebscohost.com/login.aspx?direct=true& db=bth&AN=9402182599&site=bsi-live&scope=site

Anthony, R. & Govindarajan, V., (2001). *Management control systems* (10th ed.). New York, NY: McGraw-Hill Irwin.

Askim, M. (1999). *The role of attributional explanatory style in the perceived outcomes of entrepreneurial venture failure* (Doctoral dissertation). Available from ProQuest Dissertations and Theses database. (UMI No. 730226691)

Ayres, I. (2007). *Super crunchers: Why thinking by numbers is the new way to be smart.* New York, NY: Bantam.

Babbie, E. (1973). *Survey research methods*. Belmont, CA: Wadsworth Publishing.

Backstrom, H. & Hursh-Cesar, G. (1981). *Survey research* (2nd ed.). New York, NY: Macmillan Publishing.

Ball, D., McClulloch, W., Frantz, P., Geringer, J., & Minor, M. (2006). *International business: The challenge of global competition* (10th ed.). Boston, MA: McGraw-Hill Irwin.

Barker, J.A. (1992). *Paradigms: The business of discovering the future*. New York, NY: HarperBusiness Books.

Barbosa, S., Gerhardt, M., & Kickul, J. (2007). The role of cognitive style and risk preference on entrepreneurial self-efficacy and entrepreneurial intentions. *Journal of Leadership & Organizational Studies (Baker College), 13*(4), 86-104. Retrieved from http://search.ebscohost.com/login.aspx?direct =true&db=bth&AN=25246890&site=bsi-live&scope=site

Barrese, J. (2003). Emerging trends in risk management: From the corporate consumer's perspective. *Review of Business, 24*(3), 9-10. Retrieved from http://proquest.umi.com/pqdweb?did=451021691&sid=6&Fmt=4&clie ntId=1354&RQT=309&VName=PQD

Bartlett, J. (1999). *Fundamentals of venture capital*. Lanham, MD: Madison Books.

Bates, T. (2006). The urban development potential of black-owned businesses. *American Planning Association. Journal of the American Planning Association, 72*(2), 227-237. Retrieved from http://proquest.umi.com/pqdweb ?did=1039290181&sid=1&Fmt=7&clientId=1354&RQT=309&VName =PQD

Bates, T. (2005). Analysis of young, small firms that have closed: delineating successful from unsuccessful closures. *Journal of Business Venturing, 20*(3), 343-358. Retrieved from http://proquest.umi.com/pqdweb? did=812512981&sid=Fmt=7&clientId=1354&RQT=309&VName=PQ D

Bates, T. (1998). Survival patterns among newcomers to franchising. *Journal of Business Venturing, 13*(2), 113-130. Retrieved from http://proquest. umi.com/pqdweb?did=25227795&sid=13&Fmt=2&clientId=1354&RQ T=309&VName=PQD

Bates, T., & Robb, A. (2008). Crime's impact on the survival prospects of young urban small businesses. *Economic Development Quarterly, 22*(3), 228. Retrieved from http://proquest.umi.com/pqdweb?did= 1547086831&sid=1&Fmt=7&clientId=1354&RQT=309&VName=PQ D

Beall, A. (2010). *Strategic market research: A guide to conducting research that drives Businesses*. New York, NY: iUniverse, Inc.

Beaver, W. (1966). Financial ratios as predictors of failure, *Empirical Research in Accounting, Selected Studies, 1966, Supplement to Journal of Accounting Research 4*, 71-127.

Bee, E. (2004). Small business vitality & economic development. *Economic Development Journal, 3*(3), 7-15. Retrieved from http://proquest. umi.com/pqdweb?did=729957681&sid=8&Fmt=4&clientId=1354&RQ T=309&VName=PQD

Berglund, H. K. (2005). *Toward a theory of entrepreneurial action: Exploring risk, opportunity and self in technology entrepreneurship* (Doctoral dissertation). Available from ProQuest Dissertations and Theses database. (UMI No. 1094112131)

Berkery, D., (2008). *Raising venture capital for the serious entrepreneur.* New York, NY: McGraw-Hill.

Bernstein, L., (1990). *Analysis of financial statements* (3rd ed.). Chicago, IL: Business One Irwin Publications.

Bhide, A. (1999a). The questions every entrepreneur must answer. In (Eds.) *Harvard Business Review on Entrepreneurship* (pp. 1-28). Boston, MA: Harvard Business School Press.

Bhide, A. (1999b). How entrepreneurs craft strategies that work. In (Eds.) *Harvard Business Review on Entrepreneurship* (pp. 89-16). Boston, MA: Harvard Business School Press.

Black, D. (1999). *Pyramid power: Network marketer's accounts profession development and success* (Doctoral dissertation). Available from ProQuest Dissertations and Theses database. (UMI No. 726062671)

Blakely, E.J. & Bradshaw, T.K. (2002). *Planning local economic development: theory and practice* (3rd ed.). Thousand Oaks, CA: Sage.

Bodie, Z., Kane, A. & Marcus, A. (2007). *Investments* (6th ed.). Boston, MA: McGraw-Hill Irwin.

Bonham, C., Edmonds, C., & Mak, J. (2006). The impact of 9/11 and other terrible global events on tourism in the United States and Hawaii. *Journal of Travel Research, 45*(1), 99. Retrieved from http://proquest.umi.com/ pqdweb?did=1152543841&sid=6&Fmt=2&clientId=1354&RQT=309& VName=PQD

Brandenburger, A. & Nalebuff, B. (1997). *Co-opetition: A revolution mindset that combines competition and cooperation: The game theory strategy that's changing the game of business.* New York, NY: Doubleday.

Bridges, W., (1994). *JobShift: How to prosper in the workplace without jobs.* New York, NY: Addison-Wesley.

Brown, T. (2006). *Confirmatory factor analysis for applied research.* New York, NY: Guilford Press.

Browne, K. (2001). Female entrepreneurship in the Caribbean: A multisite, pilot investigation of gender and work. *Human Organization, 60*(4), 326-342. Retrieved from http://proquest.umi.com/pqdweb?did=990440 20&sid=10&Fmt=2&clientId=1354&RQT=309&VName=PQD

Bryant, F. & Yarnold, P. (1995). Principal-components analysis and exploratory and confirmatory factor analysis. In L. Grimm & P. Yarnold (Eds.),

Reading and understanding multivariate statistics (pp. 99-134). Washington, DC: American Psychological Association.

Bryant, F. (2000). Assessing validity. In L. Grimm & P. Yarnold (Eds.), *Reading and understanding more multivariate statistics* (pp. 99-145). Washington, DC: American Psychological Association.

Bryant, M. (2004). *The portable dissertation advisor.* Thousand Oaks: CA: Corwin Press.

Bryman, A. & Cramer, D. (1990). *Quantitative data analysis for social sciences to measurement theory.* New York, NY: Routledge, Chapman and Hall.

Buffett, M. & Clark, D. (1997). *Buffettology.* New York, NY: Rawson Associates.

Buffett, W. & Cunningham, L. (2001). *The essays of Warren Buffett: Lessons for corporate America* (2nd ed.). New York, NY: University Press.

Busenitz, L. (1999). Entrepreneurial risk and strategic decision making: It's a matter of perspective. *The Journal of Applied Behavioral Science, 35*(3), 325-340. Retrieved from http://proquest.umi.com/pqdweb?did=44125296&sid=11&Fmt=2&clientId=1354&RQT=309&VName=PQD

Bygrave, W. D. (1994). *The portable MBA in entrepreneurship.* Hoboken, NJ: John Wiley & Sons.

Campbell, D. & Stanley, J. (1963). *Experimental and quasi-experimental designs for research.* Boston, MA: Houghton Mifflin.

Cantillon, R. (2001). *Essay on the nature of commerce in general* Paris, France: (A. Brewer, Trans.). [Translation of: Essai sur la nature du commerce en général]. New York, NY: Transaction Publishers. (Original work published 1732).

Caracelli, V. & Greene, J. (1997). Crafting mixed-method evaluation design. In Greene and Caracelli's (eds.), *Advances in mixed-method evaluation: The challenges and benefits of integrating diverse paradigms.* (pp. 19-32). New Directions for Program Evaluation, No. 74. San Francisco, CA: Jossey-Bass.

Carlberg, C. (1995). *Competitive business analysis with excel.* Indianapolis, IN: Business Computer Library Publications.

Carter, R. (1999). *Amway motivational organizations: Behind the smoke and mirrors.* Winter Park, FL: Backstreet Publishing.

Castrogiovanni, G., Justis, R., & Julian, S. (1993). Franchise failure rates: An assessment of magnitude and influencing factors. *Journal of Small Business Management, 31*(2), 105. Retrieved from http://proquest.umi.com/pqdweb?did=591159&Fmt=3&clientId=1354&RQT=309&VName=PQD

Cavaliere, F. & Swerdlow, M. (1988). Why franchise? *Business Forum, 13*(3), 11. Retrieved from http://proquest.umi.com/pqdweb?did=73988&Fmt=2&clientId=1354&RQT=309&VName=PQD

Chisholm, B. (1987). *The CBS color television venture: A study of failed innovation in the broadcasting industry* (Doctoral dissertation). Available from ProQuest Dissertations and Theses database. (UMI No. 749613061)

Choi, Y. R. (2001) *The early life of a new venture: An analysis of entrepreneurs' strategic decisions and stakeholders' assessments* (Doctoral dissertation). Available from ProQuest Dissertations and Theses database. (UMI No. 728982421)

Christensen, C. (1997). *The innovator's dilemma: When new technologies cause great firms to fail.* Boston, MA: Harvard School Press.

Clemens, C. (2006). Monopolistic competition and entrepreneurial risk-taking. *Economics Letters, 93*(1), 68-74. doi:10.1016/j.econlet.2006.03.050

Clemens, C., & Heinemann, M. (2006). On the Effects of Redistribution on Growth and Entrepreneurial Risk-taking. *Journal of Economics, 88*(2), 131-158. doi: 10.1007/s00712-006-0191-9

Clouse, V. G. (1986). *New venture creation—A decision based approach to entrepreneurial activity.* (Doctoral dissertation). Available from ProQuest Dissertations and Theses database. (UMI No. 752635011)

Cochran, W.G. (1963). *Sampling techniques.* Wiley Series in Probability and Mathematical Statistics-Applied: New York, NY: John Wiley & Sons.

Coelho, P. R. & McClure, J. (2004). Learning from failure. Mid – American. *Journal of Business, 20*(1), 13-20. Retrieved from http://proquest.umi.com/pqdweb?did=822999291&sid=5&Fmt=3&clientId=1354&RQT=309&VName=PQDGlobal database.

Cohn, D. (1998). *The political legacy of neoconservative rhetoric and governance: A comparative study of the impact of political leadership on consumer sentiment in Canada and the United States.* (Doctoral dissertation). Available from ProQuest Dissertations and Theses database. (UMI No. 734481361).

Coleman, A. (2001). Unidimensionality. *A Dictionary of Psychology.* Retrieved from Encyclopedia.com: http://www.encyclopedia.com/doc/1087-unidimensionality.html

Collins, T.Y. (2007). *Gender differences in entrepreneurship: A study of entrepreneurship in two Midwestern counties* (Doctoral dissertation). Available from ProQuest Dissertations and Theses database. (UMI No. 1251902611)

Converse, J. & Presser, S. (1986). *Survey questions: Handcrafting the standardized Questionnaire.* Thousand Oaks, CA: Sage.

Cooper, D. & Schindler, P. (2001). *Business research methods* (7th ed.). Boston, MA: McGraw-Hill Irwin.

Cressy, R. (2006). Why do most firms die young? *Small Business Economics, 26*(2), 103. Retrieved from http://proquest.umi.com/pqdweb?index=0&did=973216191&SrchMode=2&sid=6&Fmt=6&VInst=PROD&VType=PQD&RQT=309&VName=PQD&TS=1274805167&clientId=1354

Cunningham, M. (2005). *Organizational culture and mergers: Management's reflective perceptions of the relationship between organizational culture and a merged firm's ability to accomplish its pre-merger objectives* (Doctoral dissertation). Available from ProQuest Dissertations and Theses database. (UMI No. 920927611).

Cureton, E. & D'Agostino, R. (1993). *Factor analysis: An applied approach.* New York, NY: Psychology Press.

Da Silva, N. (2000). *An examination of owner characteristics and entrepreneurial management strategy in predicting small firm performance* (Doctoral dissertation). Available from ProQuest Dissertations and Theses database. (UMI No. 726065521)

Darlington, R., Weinberg, S. & Walberg, H. (1973). Canonical variate analysis and related techniques. *Review of Educational Research, 8*(1), 453-454.

Davies, J., Hides, M. & Powell, J. (2002). Defining the development needs of entrepreneurs in SMEs. *Education & Training, 4*(9), 406-412. Retrieved from http://proquest.umi.com/pqdweb?did=277373821&sid=7&Fmt=2&clientId=1354&RQT=309&VName=PQD

Declich, C. & Ventura, L.(2003). Consumption insurance and entrepreneurial risk: Evidence from Italian micro-data. *Journal of Economics and Finance, 27*(1), 1-18. Retrieved from http://proquest.umi.com/pqdweb?did=290677691&sid=15&Fmt=4&clientId=1354&RQT=309&VName=PQD

De Leeuw, J., Unidimensional Scaling. (March 27, 2004). Department of Statistics, *UCLA. Department of Statistics Papers.* Paper 2004032701. Retrieved from http://repositories.cdlib.org/uclastat/papers/2004032701

Dell, M. & Fredman, C. (1999). *Direct from Dell: Strategies that revolutionized an Industry.* New York, NY: Harper Business.

DeVellis, R. (1991). *Scale development: Theory and applications.* Applied Social Research Methods Series, Volume 26. Thousand Oaks, CA:

Diacon, S. (2002). Risk behavior and risk management in business life. *Journal of Risk and Insurance, 69*(2), 262-264. Retrieved from http://proquest.umi.com/pqdweb?did=124005491&sid=8&Fmt=2&clientId=1354&RQT=309&VName=PQD

Dickson, P. & Giglierano, J. (1986). Missing the boat and sinking the boat: A conceptual model of entrepreneurial risk. *Journal of Marketing, 50*(3), 58-70.

Di Gregorio, D. (2005). Re-thinking country risk: Insights from entrepreneurship theory. *International Business Review, 14*(2), 209-226. doi:0.1016/j.ibusrev.2004.04.009

DiStefano, C., Zhu, M., & Mîndrilă, D. (2009). Understanding and using factor scores: Considerations for the applied researcher, *Practical Assessment, Research & Evaluation, 14*(20), 1-11.

Dollinger, M. (1999). *Entrepreneurship: Strategies and resources* (2nd ed.). Upper Saddle River, NJ: Prentice Hall.

Drucker, P. (1958). Business objective and survival needs: notes on a discipline of business enterprise. *The Journal of Business* (pre-1986), *31*(2), 81. Retrieved from http://proquest.umi.com/pqdweb?did=386530551&sid=12&Fmt=2&clientId=1354&RQT=309&VName=PQD

Drucker, P. (1985). *Innovation & entrepreneurship.* New York, NY: Harpercollins.

Dunn-Rankin, P. (1983). *Scaling methods.* Hilllsdale, NJ: Erlbaum.

Dunn-Rankin, P., Knezek, G., Wallace, S. & Zhang, S. (2004). *Scaling methods* (2nd ed.). Hilllsdale, NJ: Erlbaum.

Edmister, R. (1972). An empirical test of financial ratio analysis for small business failure prediction. *Journal of Financial and Quantitative Analysis, 7*(2), 1477. Retrieved from http://proquest.umi.com/pqdweb? did=1166520&sid=1&Fmt=7&clientId=1354&RQT30&VName=PQD

Eggers, J. (1999). Developing entrepreneurial growth. *Ivey Business Journal, 63*(4), 76-81. Retrieved from http://proquest.umi.com/pqdweb? did=42081174&sid=1&Fmt=2&clientId=1354&RQT=309&VName=P QD

Ehrenberg, A.S. (1975). *Data reduction: Analyzing and interpreting statistical data* (4th ed.). New York, NY: John Wiley & Sons.

Everett, J. & Watson, J. (1998). Small business failures and external risk factors. *Small Business Economics, 11*(4), 371-390. Retrieved from http:// proquest.umi.com/pqdweb?did=41639655&sid=2&Fmt=2&clientId=13 54&RQT=309&VName=PQD

Farris, P., Bendle, N., Pfeifer, P., & Reibstein, D. (2006). *The marketing metrics: 50+ metrics every executive should master.* Upper Saddle River, NJ: Wharton School Publishing.

Fiet, J. & Patel, P. (2006). Evaluating the wealth-creating potential of business plans. *The Journal of Private Equity, 10*(1), 18-32. Retrieved from http:// proquest.umi.com/pqdweb?did=1188972821&sid=3&Fmt=2&clientId= 1354&RQT=309&VName=PQD

Field, A., (2005). *Discovering statistics using SPSS* (2nd ed.). Thousand Oaks, CA: Sage.

Ferriss, T. (2007). *The 4-hour workweek: Escape 9-5, live anywhere and join the new rich.* New York, NY: Crown Publishers.

Fink, A. (2006). *How to conduct surveys* (3rd ed.). Thousand Oaks, CA: Sage.

Fitzpatrick, P. (1931). *Symptoms of industrial failures.* Washington, DC: Catholic University Press.

Fitzpatrick, P. (1932). Symptoms comparison of the ratios successful industrial enterprises with those failed companies, Washington, DC: *The Accountants Publishing Co.*

Fitzpatrick, R. & Reynolds, J. (1997). *False profits: Seeking financial and spiritual deliverance in multi-level marketing and pyramid schemes.* Charlotte, NC: Herald Press.

Foreman-Peck, J., Makepeace, G., & Morgan, B. (2006). Growth and profitability of small and medium-sized enterprises: Some Welsh evidence. *Regional Studies, 40*(4), 307-320. doi:10.1080/00343400600725160

Forlani, D. & Mullins, J. (2001). Market entry strategies of successful entrepreneurs: The effects of risk propensity and risk perceptions. *American Marketing Association. Conference Proceedings:* 2001 AMA Winter Educators' Conference: Marketing Theory, 12, 364. Retrieved from

http://proquest.umi.com/pqdweb?did=72792740&sid=5&Fmt=3&clien
tId=1354&RQT=309&VName=PQD

Forlani, D. & Mullins, J. (2000). Perceived risks and choices in entrepreneurs' new venture decisions. *Journal of Business Venturing, 15*(4), 305-322. Retrieved from http://proquest.umi.com/pqdweb?did=55643103&sid=4& Fmt=2&clientId=1354&RQT=309&VName=PQD

Formani, R. (2001). The engine of capitalist process: Entrepreneurs in economic theory, *Economic & Financial Review*. 2-11. Retrieved from http://proquest.umi.com/pqdweb?did=113031073&sid=9&Fmt=2&clie ntId=1354&RQT=309&VName=PQD

Fox, D. (2009, January). Government Policies and Entrepreneurship. D.T. Smith (Facilitator) *Risk in the economy for entrepreneurs and industries.* Symposium workshop conducted at the meeting of the 2009 United States Associations of Small Business and Entrepreneurship (USASBE) Conference Proceedings, Anaheim, California.

Fowler, F. (1988). *Survey research methods.* Applied Social Research Methods Series, Volume 1. Thousand Oaks, CA: Sage.

Fowler, F. (1995). *Improving survey questions: Design and evaluation.* Applied Social Research Methods Series, Volume 38. Thousand Oaks, CA: Sage.

Fridson, M. (2000). *How to be a billionaire: Proven strategies from the titans of wealth.* New York, NY: John Wiley & Sons.

Fritz, D. (2006). *Entrepreneurial behaviors and performance: An empirical investigation into the components of entrepreneurial orientation and their impacts and interactions with environmental munificence and performance in a non-profit context* (Doctoral dissertation). Available from ProQuest Dissertations and Theses database. (UMI No. 1221692761)

Gadsden, E. (2000). *From traditional cabinetmaking to entrepreneurial production: David Evans (1748--1819)* (Doctoral dissertation). Available from ProQuest Dissertations and Theses database. (UMI No. 732163701)

Gahin, F. (1967). A theory of pure risk management in the business firm. *Journal of Risk and Insurance* (pre-1986), *34*(1), 121. Retrieved from http://proquest.umi.com/pqdweb?did=677825141&sid=6&Fmt=2&clie ntId=1354&RQT=309&VName=PQD

Gallik, J. S. (1989). *Factors contributing to the emergence of an intrapreneurial event, and an exploratory study of organizational learning in ecological configurations* (Doctoral dissertation). Available from ProQuest Dissertations and Theses database. (UMI No. 745828101)

Galindo, M., Escribano-Sotos, F. & Méndez-Picazo, M. (2007). Value at risk and economic growth. *International Advances in Economic Research, 13*(2), 214.doi:10.1007/s11294-006-9060-0

Garson, D. (1998). Factor analysis. Retrieved from http://faculty.chass.ncsu. edu/garson/PA765/factor.htm#factoring

Gaskill, L., Van Auken, H., & Manning, R. (1993). A factor analytic study of the perceived causes of small business failure. *Journal of Small Business*

Management, 31(4), 18. Retrieved from http://proquest.umi.com/pqdweb?did=738987&sid=5&Fmt=3&clientId=1354&RQT=309&VName=PQD

George, D. & Mallery, P. (2003). *SPSS for Windows step by step: A simple guide and reference 11.0 update* (4th ed.). Boston, MA: Allyn and Bacon.

Gerber, M. E. (1995). *The e-myth revisited: Why most small businesses don't work and what to do about it.* New York, NY: Harper Business.

Giles, S. & Blakely, E. (2001). *Fundamentals of economic development finance.* Thousand Oaks, CA: Sage.

Gilmore, A., Carson, D. & O'Donnell, A. (2004). Small business owner-managers and their attitude to risk. *Marketing Intelligence & Planning, 22*(2/3), Retrieved from http://proquest.umi.com/pqdweb?did=656758981&sid=9&Fmt=2&clientId=1354&RQT=309&VName=PQD

Glenberg, A. (1996). *Learning from data: An introduction to statistical reasoning* (2nd ed.). Mahwah, NJ: Lawrence Erlbaum Associates

Goldratt, E. (1990). *Theory of constraints.* Great Barrington, MA: North River Press.

Golis, C. (2002). *Enterprise & venture capital: A business builder's and investor's handbook* (4th ed.). Crows Nest, Australia: Allen & Unwin.

Gorden, R. (1977). *Unidimensional scaling of social variables: Concepts and procedures.* New York, NY: Free Press.

Gordon, M. (2007). *Trump university: Entrepreneurship 101.* New York, NY: John Wiley and Sons Press.

Gorsuch, R. (1983). *Factor analysis* (2nd ed.). Hillsdale, NJ: Erlbaum.

Graham, B. (2003a). *The intelligent investor-revised edition* (2nd ed.). New York, NY: HarperCollins Publishers-First Collins Business Essentials. (Original work published 1949) (pp. 204-205; 212-215).

Graham, B. (2003b). *The interpretation of financial statements* (2nd ed.). New York, NY: HarperCollins Publishers-HarperBusiness. (Original work published 1937).

Green, S., Salkind, N. & Akey, T. (2000). *Using SPSS for Windows: Analyzing and understanding data* (2nd ed.). Upper Saddle River, NJ: Prentice-Hall.

Grice, J. (2001). Computing and evaluating factor scores. *Psychological Methods, 6*(4), 430-450. doi:10.1037//1082-989X.6.4.430

Gutter, M. & Saleem, T. (2005). Financial vulnerability of small business owners. *Financial Services Review, 14*(2), 133-147. Retrieved from http://proquest.umi.com/pqdweb?did=857337441&sid=10&Fmt=2&clientId=1354&RQT=309&VName=PQD

Hamilton, B. H. (2000). Does entrepreneurship pay? An empirical analysis of the returns to self-employment. *The Journal of Political Economy, 108*(3), 604-631. Retrieved from http://proquest.umi.com/pqdweb?did=54856643&sid=11&Fmt=2&clientId=1354&RQT=309&VName=PQD

Hair, J., Anderson, R., Tatham, R. & Black, W. (1998). *Multivariate data analysis with reading* (5th ed.). Englewood Cliffs, NJ: Prentice-Hall.

Harman, H. (1976). *Modern factor analysis* (3rd ed.). Chicago, IL: University of Chicago Press.

Harris, D. (1992). *Pyramid power: Of profits and prophecy: A study of the Amway Worldwide* (Doctoral dissertation). Available from ProQuest Dissertations and Theses database. (UMI No. 747183651)

Harting, T. (2005). *The cost of failure: An empirical look at the financial effect of business failure on the self-employed* (Doctoral dissertation). Available from ProQuest Dissertations and Theses database. (UMI No. 994230071)

Hatala, J. (2005). identifying barriers to self-employment: The development and validation of the barriers to entrepreneurship success tool. *Performance Improvement Quarterly, 18*(4), 50-70. Retrieved from ABI/INFORM Global database. (Document ID: 983631191).

Headd, B. (2003). Redefining business success: Distinguishing between closure and failure. *Small Business Economics, 21*(1), 51-61. Retrieved from http://proquest.umi.com/pqdweb?did=410459781&sid=12&Fmt=2&clientId=1354&RQT=309&VName=PQD

Hickman, W. B. (1958). *Corporate bond quality and investor experience.* Princeton, NJ: Princeton University Press.

Hildebrando, V. (2003). *Assessing entrepreneurial characteristics in a Brazilian training program* (Doctoral dissertation). Available from ProQuest Dissertations and Theses database. (UMI No. 765345961)

Hirschey, M. & Pappas, J. (1992). *Fundamentals of managerial economics* (4th ed.). Fort Worth, TX: The Dryden Press.

Hirschey, M. (2006). *Managerial economics* (11th ed.). Mason, OH: Thomson South-Western.

Hoff, K. (1989). *Three essays in the theory of trade and taxation under incomplete risk Markets* (Doctoral dissertation). Available from ProQuest Dissertations and Theses database. (UMI No. 745315481)

Hollman, K. & Mohammad-Zadeh, S. (1984). Risk management in small business. *Journal of Small Business Management, 22* (1), 47-55.

Horrigan, J. (1966). The determination of long-term credit standing with financial ratios, *Empirical Research in Accounting, Selected Studies 1966, Supplement to Journal of Accounting Research 4* (1), 44-62.

Huck, S., Cormier, W. & Bounds, W. (1974). *Reading statistics and research.* New York, NY: Harper & Row.

Hugos, M. (2003). *Essentials of supply chain management.* Upper Saddle River, NJ: John Wiley and Sons.

Hunt, N. & Tyrell, S. (2001). The advantages and disadvantages of stratified sampling. *Stratified Sampling.* Retrieved from Encyclopedia.com: http://www.coventry.ac.uk/ec/~nhunt/meths/strati.html

Hunter, I. (2005). Risk, persistence and focus: a life cycle of the entrepreneur. *Australian Economic History Review, 45*(3), 244-272.

Huyghebaert, N. & Van De Gucht, L. (2004). Incumbent strategic behavior in financial and the exit of entrepreneurial start-ups. *Strategic Management Journal, 25*(7), 669-688. doi:10.1002/smj.415

Isaac, S. & Michael, W. (1982). *Handbook in research and evaluation* (2nd ed.). San Diego, CA: EdITs Publishers.

Ireland, R. D., Kuratko, D. & Morris, M. (2006). A health audit for corporate entrepreneurship: Innovation at all levels: Part I. *The Journal of Business Strategy, 27*(1), 10-17. Retrieved from http://proquest.umi.com/pqdweb?did=1005035561&sid=13&Fmt=2&clientId=1354&RQT=309&VName=PQD

Iyigun, M., & Owen, A. (1998). Risk, entrepreneurship, and human-capital accumulation. *American Economic Review, 88*(2), 454-457.

Jaccard, J. & Jacoby, J. (2010). *Theory construction and model-building skills: A practical guide for social scientists.* New York, NY: The Guildford Press.

Jarillo-Mossi, J. (1986) *Entrepreneurial and growth: the strategic use of external resourses* (Doctoral dissertation). Available from ProQuest Dissertations and Theses database. (UMI No. 752978151)

Janney, J. & Dess, G. (2006). The risk concept for entrepreneurs reconsidered: New challenges to the conventional wisdom. *Journal of Business Venturing, 21*(3), 385-400. Retrieved from http://proquest.umi.com/pqdweb?did=1014905571&sid=1&Fmt=7&clientId=1354&RQT=309&VName=PQD

Jeannet, J. & Hennessey, H.D. (2001). *Global marketing: An interactive approach* (5th ed.). Boston, MA: South-Western College.

Johnson, C. R. (1998). *CEO logic.* Franklin Lakes, NJ: Career Press.

Jones, R. (1996). *Research methods in the social and behavioral sciences* (2nd ed.). Sunderland, MA: Sinauer Associates.

Joseph, R., Nekoranec, A. & Steffens, C., (1993). *How to buy a business.* Chicago, IL: Enterprise-Dearborn.

Kachigan, S. (1991). *Multivariate statistical methods: A conceptual approach* (2nd ed.). New York, NY: Radius Press.

Kachigan, S. (1986). *Statistical analysis: An interdisciplinary introduction to univariate & multivariate methods.* New York, NY: Radius Press.

Kanbur, S. & Ravi, M. (1982). Entrepreneurial risk taking, inequality, and public policy: An application of inequality decomposition analysis to the general equilibrium effects of progressive taxation. *The Journal of Political Economy, 90*(1), 1. Retrieved from ABI/INFORM Global database. (Document ID: 1179439).

Kaplan, R. & Norton, D. (1996). *The balanced scorecard: Translating strategy into action.* Boston, MA: Harvard Business Press.

Kazem, A. (2003). *Competitiveness of SMEs: The influence of entrepreneur's characteristics and firm's operational strategies: Case study of Egypt* (Doctoral dissertation). Available from ProQuest Dissertations and Theses database. (UMI No. 765378091)

Keegan, W. & Green, M. (1997). *Principles of global marketing.* Upper Saddle River, NJ: Prentice-Hall.

Kennedy, D. (2001). *Loop-holes of the rich.* New York, NY: Warner Business Books.

Keppel, G. (1982). *Design and analysis: A researcher's handbook* (2nd ed.). Englewood Cliffs, NJ: Prentice-Hall.

Kerlinger, F. (1985). *Foundations of behavioral research* (3rd ed.). New York, NY: Holt Rinehart and Winston.

Kerlinger, F. & Pedhazur, E. (1973). *Multiple regression in behavioral research,* New York, NY: Holt, Rinehart and Winston.

Khavul, S. (2001). *Money and knowledge: Sources of seed capital and the performance of high-technology start-ups* (Doctoral dissertation). Available from ProQuest Dissertations and Theses database. (UMI No. 728446081)

Kim J. & Mueller, C. (1978a). *Introduction to factor analysis: What it is and how to do it.* Quantitative Applications in the Social Sciences Series, No.13. Thousand Oaks, CA: Sage.

Kim J. & Mueller, C. (1978b). *Factor analysis: Statistical methods and practical issues.* Quantitative Applications in the Social Sciences Series, No.14. Thousand Oaks, CA: Sage.

Kish, L. (1987). *Statistical design for research.* New York, NY: Wiley Series in Probability and Mathematical Statistics-Applied: John Wiley & Sons.

Kiyosaki, R. & Lechter, S. (1999). *Cashflow quadrant* (2nd ed.). New York, NY: Warner Business Books.

Kline, R. (1998). *Principles and practices of structural equation modeling.* New York, NY: The Guilford Press.

Knopper, S. (2009). *Appetite for self-destruction: The spectacular crash of the record industry in the digital age.* New York, NY: Free Press.

Knott, A. & Posen, H. (2005). Is failure good? *Strategic Management Journal, 26*(7), 617+. Retrieved from http://proquest.umi.com/pqdweb?did=857254891&sid=14&Fmt=2&clientId=1354&RQT=309&VName=PQD

Koch, R. (2003). *The 80/20 individual.* New York, NY: Currency-Doubleday.

Kotler, P. & Keller, K. (2009). *A framework for marketing management.* Upper Saddle River, NJ: Prentice Hall.

Krueger, D. (1998). Personality characteristics of the small business entrepreneur. *Journal of Business and Entrepreneurship, 10*(1), 26-0. 10. Retrieved from http://proquest.umi.com/pqdweb?did=1396123491&sid=8&Fmt=4&clientId=1354&RQT=309&VName=PQD

Kuntze, R. (2001). *Pyramid power: The dark side of multi-level marketing: Appeals to the symbolically incomplete* (Doctoral dissertation). Available from ProQuest Dissertations and Theses database. (UMI No. 728469091)

Kuratko, D., Hornsby, J. & Naffziger, D. (1997). An examination of owner's goals in sustaining entrepreneurship. *Journal of Small Business Management, 35*(1), 24-33. Retrieved from http://proquest.umi.com/pqdweb?

did=11286966&sid=15&Fmt=4&clientId=1354&RQT=309&VName= PQD

Kuratko, D. & Ireland, R. & Hornsby, J. (2001). Improving firm performance through entrepreneurial actions: Acordia's corporate entrepreneurship strategy. *The Academy of Management Executive, 15*(4), 60-71. Retrieved from http://proquest.umi.com/pqdweb?did=105262907&sid=16&Fmt =2&clientId=1354&RQT=309&VName=PQD

Lambing, P. & Kuehl, C. (2007). *Entrepreneurship* (3rd ed.). Upper Saddle River, NJ: Prentice Hall.

Lechter, M. (2001). *Protecting your #1 asset* (2nd ed.). New York, NY: Warner Business Books.

Leeb, S. & Strathy, G. (2006). *The coming economic collapse: How you can thrive when oil Costs $200 a barrel.* New York, NY: Warner Business Books.

Leedy, P. & Ormrod, J. (2001). *Practical research: Planning and design* (7th ed.). Upper Saddle River, NJ: Merrill Prentice Hall.

Leyden, D. & Link., N. (2004). Transmission of risk-averse behavior in small firms. *Small Business Economics, 23*(3), 255. Retrieved from http:// proquest.umi.com/pqdweb?did=660139371&sid=17&Fmt=2&clientId= 1354&RQT=309&VName=PQD

Littunen, H. (2000). Entrepreneurship and the characteristics of the entrepreneurial personality. *International Journal of Entrepreneurial Behavior & Research, 6*(6), 295. Retrieved from http://proquest.umi.com/pqdweb? did=117540040&sid=18&Fmt=2&clientId=1354&RQT=309&VName =PQD

Long, T., Convey, J. & Chwalek, A. (1985). *Completing dissertations in the behavioral sciences and education.* San Francisco, CA: Jossey-Bass.

Long, J. S. (1983). *Confirmatory factor analysis.* Quantitative Applications in the Social Sciences Series, No. 33. Thousand Oaks, CA: Sage.

Longenecker, J., Moore, C., Petty, J. & Palich, L. (2006). *Small business management: An entrepreneurial emphasis* (13th ed.). New Jersey: Thomson-Southwester.

Lowenstein, R., (1995). *Buffett: The making of an American capitalist.* New York, NY: Random House.

Lumpkin, G. (1996). *The entrepreneurial orientation (EO) of new entrants: Performance implications of alternative configurations of EO, environment, and structure* (Doctoral dissertation). Available from ProQuest Dissertations and Theses database. (UMI No. 743155821)

Luo, Y. (2005). *Essays on macroeconomics with microeconomic* (Doctoral dissertation). Available from ProQuest Dissertations and Theses database. (UMI No.885694411)

Macias, K. (2000). *A financial audit model for entrepreneurial governments* (Doctoral dissertation). Available from ProQuest Dissertations and Theses database. (UMI No. 728845431)

Mainprize, B. & Hindle, K. (2005). Assessing the efficacy and standardization potential of five competing venture capital investment evaluation approaches. *The Journal of Private Equity, 9*(1), 6-21. Retrieved from http://proquest.umi.com/pqdweb?did=954037531&sid=19&Fmt=2&clientId=1354&RQT=309&VName=PQD

Mariotti, S. (2007). *Entrepreneurship: Starting and operating a small business.* Upper Saddle River, NJ: Pearson –Prentice Hall.

Martín, G., Sotos, F., & Picazo, M. (2007). Value at risk and economic growth. *International Advances in Economic Research,* 13(2), 214.doi: 10.1007/s11294-006-9060-0

McAuley, J., (1986). *Forecasting for business: Concepts and application.* Englewood Cliffs, NJ: Prentice-Hall, Inc.

McClave, J. & Sincich T., (2003). *Statistics* (9th ed.). Upper Saddle River, NJ: Prentice Hall.

McCormack, M. (1984). *What they don't teach you at Harvard Business School.* New York, NY: Bantam Books.

McInerney, F. & White, S. (2000). *FutureWealth.* New York, NY: St. Martin's Press.

McKnight, L., Vaaler, P., & Katz, R (2001). *Creative destruction: Business survival strategies in the global internet economy.* Cambridge, MA: MIT Press.

Megginson, L., Byrd, M., & Megginson, W. (2003). *Small business management: An entrepreneur's guidebook* (4th ed.). Boston, MA: McGraw-Hill Irwin.

Menefee, M. & Parnell, J. (2007). Factors associated with success and failure among firms in high technology environments: A research note. *Journal of Applied Management and Entrepreneurship, 12*(4), 60-73. Retrieved from http://proquest.umi.com/pqdweb?did=1429487841&sid=21&Fmt=2&clientId=1354&RQT=309&VName=PQD

Merriam-Webster Collegiate Dictionary (9th ed.). (1984). Springfield, MA: Merriam-Webster.

Merwin, C. (1942). Financing small corporations: In five manufacturing industries, 1926-36, *National Bureau of Economic Research.* 1- 56.

Miaoulis, G., Brown, H., & Saunders, P. (2005). Perceptions of environmental restraints on start-ups in Southwestern Pennsylvania. *The Journal of Business and Economic Studies, 11*(2), 19-33; 91-92. Retrieved from http://proquest.umi.com/pqdweb?did=976374471&sid=20&Fmt=2&clientId=1354&RQT=309&VName=PQD

Michael, S. & Combs, J. (2008). Entrepreneurial failure: The case of franchisees. *Journal of Small Business Management, 46*(1), 73-90. Retrieved from http://proquest.umi.com/pqdweb?did=1427433431&sid=22&Fmt=2&clientId=1354&RQT=309&VName=PQD

Miles, D. (2006, January). *New venture matrix: A risk assessment tool for new business startup ventures.* In Y.A. Hegazy (Chair). USASBE small business workshop session. Symposium workshop conducted at the meeting of the 2006 United States Associations of Small Business and Entrepreneurship (USASBE) Conference Proceedings, Tucson, Arizona.

Miles, M. & Darroch, J. (2006). Large firms, entrepreneurial marketing processes, and the cycle of competitive advantage. *European Journal of Marketing*, *40*(5/6), 485-501. Retrieved from http://proquest.umi.com/pqdweb?did=1131526491&sid=23&Fmt=2&clientId=1354&RQT=309&VName=PQD

Miles, R., Snow, C., & Meyer, A. (1978). Organizational strategy, structure, and process. *Academy of Management: The Academy of Management Review*, *3*(3), 546. Retrieved from http://proquest.umi.com/pqdweb?did=944497&sid=24&Fmt=2&clientId=1354&RQT=309&VName=PQD

Mohammad-Zadeh, S. (1984). Entrepreneurial risk taking in family firms. *Journal of Small Business Management*, *22* (1), 47-55.

Morgan, S., Reichert, T., & Harrison, T. (2002). *From numbers to words: reporting statistical results for the social sciences*. Boston, MA: Allyn & Bacon

Moss, S., Ryan, C., & Moss, J. (2006). The life cycle of a terrorism crisis: impact on tourist travel. *Allied Academies International Conference. Academy of Strategic Management. Proceedings*, *5*(2), 1. Retrieved from http://proquest.umi.com/pqdweb?did=1560736291&sid=8&Fmt=3&clientId=1354&RQT=309&VName=PQD

Mossi, J. (1986). *Entrepreneurship and growth: the strategic use of external resources* (Doctoral dissertation). Available from ProQuest Dissertations and Theses database. (UMI No. 752978151)

Motl, R., Dishman, R., Dowda, M., & Pate, R. (2004). Factorial validity and invariance of a self-report measure of physical activity among adolescent girls, *Research Quarterly for Exercise and Sport*, *32*(1), 1-25.

Mulaik, S. (1972). *Foundations of factor analysis* (2nd ed.). New York, NY: Chapman & Hall Publishing.

Murphy, P., Liao, J. & Welsch, H., (2006). A conceptual history of entrepreneurial thought. *Journal of Management History*, *12*(1), 12. Retrieved from http://proquest.umi.com/pqdweb?did=1074205241&sid=25&Fmt=2&clientId=1354&RQT=309&VName=PQD

Neff, G.S. (2004). *Organizing uncertainty: Individual, organizational and institutional risk in New York's Internet industry, 1995-2003* (Doctoral dissertation). Available from ProQuest Dissertations and Theses database. (UMI No. 765350021)

Newman, A. (2007). Risk-bearing and entrepreneurship. *Journal of Economic Theory*, *137*(1), 11-26. doi:10.1016/j.jet.2007.03.004.

Newton, R. & Rudestam, K. (1999). *Your statistical consultant: Answers to your data analysis questions*. Thousand Oaks, CA: Sage.

Nichol, A. & Pexman, P. (2000). *Presenting your findings: A practical guide for creating tables* (6th ed.). Washington, DC: American Psychological Association.

Norton Jr., W. & Moore, W. T. (2002). Entrepreneurial risk: Have we been asking the wrong question? *Small Business Economics*, *18*(4), 281-287. Retrieved from http://proquest.umi.com/pqdweb? did=124172061&sid= 26&Fmt=2&clientId=1354&RQT=309&VName=PQD

Norton Jr., W. & Moore, W. T. (2006). The influence of entrepreneurial risk assessment on venture launch or growth decisions. *Small Business Economics, 26*(3), 215. Retrieved from http://proquest.umi.com/pqdweb? did=993032791&sid=27&Fmt=2&clientId=1354&RQT=309&VName= PQD

O'Neill, H. & Duker, J. (1986). Survival and failure in small business. *Journal of Small Business Management, 24*(1), 30. 15-35. Retrieved from http://proquest.umi.com/pqdweb?did=1186526&Fmt=2&clientId=135 4&RQT=309&VName=P

Osborne, R. (1993). Why entrepreneurs fail: How to avoid the traps. *Management Decision, 31*(1), 18. Retrieved from http://proquest. umi.com/pqdweb?did=603105&sid=28&Fmt=2&clientId=1354&RQT =309&VName=PQD

Oster, S. (1990). *Modern competition analysis*. New York, NY: Oxford Press Publishers.

Panousi, V. (2008). *Essays in incomplete markets. Ph.D. dissertation* (Doctoral dissertation). Available from ProQuest Dissertations and Theses database. (UMI No. 1597600281)

Parhankangas, A., & Hellström, T. (2007). How experience and perceptions shape risky behaviour: Evidence from the venture capital industry. *Venture Capital, 9*(3), 183-205. doi:10.1080/13691060701324478

Pardo, C. (2005). *Risk aversion, private information and real fluctuations* (Doctoral dissertation). Available from ProQuest Dissertations and Theses database. (UMI No. 982807701)

Parsa, G., Self, J., Njite, D., & King, T. (2005). Why Restaurants Fail. *Cornell Hotel and Restaurant Administration Quarterly, 46*(3), 304-322. Retrieved from http://proquest.umi.com/pqdweb?index=0&did=878036131&Sr chMode=2&sid=8&Fmt=4&VInst=PROD&VType=PQD&RQT=309 &VName=PQD&TS=1285781823&clientId=1354

Peterson, R. Kozmetsky, G., & Ridgway, N. (1983). Perceived causes of small business failures: A research note. *American Journal of Small Business, 8*(1), 15. 76-95. Retrieved from http://proquest.umi.com/pqdweb? did=951052&sid=1&Fmt=7&clientId=1354&RQT=309&VName=PQ D

Petrakis, P. (2004). Entrepreneurship and risk premium. *Small Business Economics, 23*(2), 85-98. Retrieved from http://proquest.umi.com/pqdweb? did=642290191&sid=29&Fmt=2&clientId=1354&RQT=309&VName= PQD

Petrakis, P. (2005a). Growth, entrepreneurship, structural change, time and risk. *Journal of American Academy of Business*, Cambridge, *7*(1), 243-250. Retrieved from http://proquest.umi.com/pqdweb? did=850335121&sid= 30&Fmt=2&clientId=1354&RQT=309&VName=PQD

Petrakis, P. (2005b). Risk perception, risk propensity and entrepreneurial behavior: The Greek case. *Journal of American Academy of Business*, Cambridge, *7*(1), 233-242. Retrieved from http://proquest.umi.com/pqdweb?did=850335371&sid=31&Fmt=2&clientId=1354&RQT=309&VName=PQD

Phillips, F. & Garman, A. (2005). Barriers to entrepreneurship in healthcare organizations. *Journal of Health and Human Services Administration, 28*(3/4), 472-484; 463; 465. Retrieved from http://proquest.umi.com/pqdweb?did=1007951011&sid=1&Fmt=3&clientId=1354&RQT=309&VName=PQD

Porter, M. (1985). *The competitive advantage: Creating and sustaining superior performance*. New York, NY: Simon & Schuster.

Porter, M. (1989). *Competitive strategy: Techniques for analyzing industries and competitors*. New York, NY: Free Press.

Porter, M. (1990). *The competitive advantage of nations*. New York, NY: Free Press.

Psaltopoulos, D., Stathopoulou, S. & Skuras, D. (2005). The location of markets, perceived entrepreneurial risk, and start-up capital of micro rural firms, *Small Business Economics, 25*(2), 147-158.

Pulley, B. (2004). *The billion dollar BET*. Hoboken, NJ: John Wiley.

Rampini, A. (2004). Entrepreneurial activity, risk, and the business cycle. *Journal of Monetary Economics, 51*(3), 555-573. Retrieved from http://proquest.umi.com/pqdweb?did=666886851&sid=1&Fmt=7&clientId=1354&R QT=309&VName=PQD

Raubenheimer, J. (2004). An item selection procedure to maximize scale reliability and validity. *South African Journal of Industrial Psychology, 30* (4), 59-64.

Richards, R. M. (1984). Meeting the challenge of entrepreneurial risk. *Risk Management, 31*(5), 22. Retrieved from http://proquest.umi.com/pqdweb?did=1299367&sid=32&Fmt=2&clientId=1354&RQT=309&VName=PQD

Ricketts, L., Gaskill, H., Van Auken, H., & Manning, R. (1993). A factor analytic study of the perceived causes of small business failure. *Journal of Small Business Management, 11*(4), 18-31.

Robb, A. (2002). Entrepreneurial performance by women and minorities: The case of new firms. *Journal of Developmental Entrepreneurship, 7*(4), 383-397. Retrieved from http://proquest.umi.com/pqdweb?did=283036131&sid=33&Fmt=2&clientId=1354&RQT=309&VName=PQD

Rodriguez, L. T. (2000). *The wind beneath their wings: The moderating effects of social support on the entrepreneur and entrepreneurial performance outcomes* (Doctoral dissertation). Available from ProQuest Dissertations and Theses database. (UMI No. 727706361)

Rose, J. (2002, March). The new risk takers. *FSB: Fortune Small Business, 12*(2), 28-34. Retrieved from http://proquest.umi.com/pqdweb?did=110701005&sid=34&Fmt=2&clientId=1354&RQT=309&VName=PQD

Roussanov, N. (2008). *Diversification and its discontents: Idiosyncratic and entrepreneurial risk in the quest for social status* (Doctoral dissertation). Available from ProQuest Dissertations and Theses database. (UMI No. 1472138611)

Rummel, R. J. (1970). *Applied factor analysis.* Evanston, NJ: Northwestern University Press.

Runyan, C. (2006). Small business in the face of crisis: identifying barriers to recovery from a natural disaster. *Journal of Contingencies and Crisis Management, 14*(1), 1. doi:10.1111/j.1468-5973.2006.00477.x

Runyan, R. & Huddleston, P. (2006). Getting customers downtown: the role of branding in achieving success for central business districts. *The Journal of Product and Brand Management, 15*(1), 48-61. Retrieved from http://proquest.umi.com/pqdweb?did=1036182071&sid=1&Fmt=7&clientId=1354&RQT=309&VName=PQD

Sandino, T. (2004). *Introducing the first management control systems: Evidence from the retail sector* (Doctoral dissertation). Available from ProQuest Dissertations and Theses database. (UMI No. 920923731)

Santarelli, E. & Vivarelli, M. (2007). Entrepreneurship and the process of firms' entry, survival and growth. *Industrial and Corporate Change, 16*(3), 455-488. Retrieved from http://proquest.umi.com/pqdweb?did=1317779661&sid=35&Fmt=2&clientId=1354&RQT=309&VName=PQD

Schenk, C. (2002). Banding together for SME credit risk analytics. *Risk, 15* (11), 24-26.

Schumpter, J.A. (1975), *Capitalism, socialism and democracy* (4th ed) New York, NY: Harper, [orig. pub. 1942].

Selig, G. (1998). Franchising and entrepreneurship: High reward or high risk? *New England Journal of Entrepreneurship, 1*(1), 13. Retrieved from http://proquest.umi.com/pqdweb?did=310961121&Fmt=4&clientId=1354&RQT=309&VName=PQD

Selltiz, C., Jahoda, M., Deutsch, M., & Cook, S. (1951). *Research methods in social sciences.* New York, NY: Holt, Rinehart and Winston Publications.

Shane, S. (2005). *Finding fertile ground: Identifying extraordinary opportunities for new ventures.* Upper Saddle River, NJ: Wharton School Publishing.

Shane, S. (2008). *The illusions of entrepreneurship,* New Haven, CT: Yale University Press.

Shane, S. & Foo, M. (1999). New firm survival: Institutional explanations for new franchisor mortality. *Management Science, 45*(2), 142-159. Retrieved from http://proquest.umi.com/pqdweb?did=40466329& Fmt=4& clientId=1354&RQT=309&VName=PQD

Sherman, A.(1999). *Franchising and licensing: Two ways to build your business* (2nd ed.). New York, NY: Amacom Publications.

Sherman, P. (2004). *The impact of realistic entrepreneurship previews on entrepreneurial biases, risk perception and opportunity evaluation* (Doctoral dissertation). Available from ProQuest Dissertations and Theses database. (UMI No. 790242431)

Slater, W. (2003). *The Wal-mart decade: How a new generation of leaders turned Sam Walton's legacy into the world's #1 company,* New York, NY: Portfolio.

Slywotzky, A., Morrison, D., & Andelman, B. (2002). *The profit zone: How strategic business designs will lead you to tomorrow's profits.* New York, NY: Three Rivers Press.

Slywotzky, A., Morrison, D., Andelman, B., Moser, T., Mundt, K., & Quella, J. (1999). *Profit patterns: 30 ways anticipate and profit from strategic forces reshaping your Business.* New York, NY: Time Business.

Small Business Administration (SBA) (2007). *Summary of size standards by industry.* Retrieved from: http://www.sba.gov/contractingopportunities/officials/size/summaryofssi/index.html

Small business at risk. (2002). *Australian CPA, 72* (9), 12, 3-4. Retrieved March 3, 2008 from http://search.ebscohost.com/login.aspx?direct=true&db=bth&AN=7902450&site=bsi-live&scope=site.

Song, M. (1983). *Successful Korean businesses in the United States – A study of excellence* (Doctoral dissertation). Available from ProQuest Dissertations and Theses database. (UMI No. 749381691)

Spearman, C. (1904). General intelligence, objectively determined and measured. *American Journal of Psychology, 15*(4), pp. 201-293.

Spector, R. (2003). *Category killers: The retail revolution and its impact on consumer culture.* Boston, MA: Harvard Business School Press.

St-Pierre, J. & Bahri, M. (2006). The use of the accounting beta as an overall risk indicator for unlisted companies. *Journal of Small Business and Enterprise Development, 13*(4), 546-561. Retrieved from http://proquest.umi.com/pqdweb?did=1164911211&sid=36&Fmt=2&clientId=1354&RQT=309&VName=PQD

Stanley, T. & Danko, W. (1996). *The millionaire next door.* Atlanta, GA: Longstreet Press.

Stanley, T. (2001). *The millionaire mind.* Atlanta, GA: Longstreet Press.

Stewart, W., Carland, J., Watson, W. & Sweo, R. (2003). Entrepreneurial dispositions and goal orientations: A comparative exploration of United States and Russian entrepreneurs. *Journal of Small Business Management, 41*(1), 27-46. Retrieved from http://proquest.umi.com/pqdweb?did=283866921&sid=37&Fmt=2&clientId=1354&RQT=309&VName=PQD

Sutton, G. (2003). *How to buy & sell a business.* New York, NY: Warner Business Books.

Strotmann, H. (2007). *Entrepreneurial survival small business economics, 28*(1), 84-101. Retrieved from http://proquest.umi.com/pqdweb?did=1193325671&sid=38&Fmt=2&clientId=1354&RQT=309&VName=PQD

Sull, D. (2005). *Made in China: What western managers can learn from trailblazing Chinese entrepreneurs.* Boston, MA: Harvard Business School Press.

Sutton, G. (2001). *Own your own corporation.* New York, NY: Warner Business Books.

Tabachnick, B & Fidell, L. (2007). *Using multivariate statistics* (5th ed.). Boston, MA: Pearson.

Taliento, M. (2007). The role and the ambit of corporate governance and risk control frames. *Journal of American Academy of Business, 11*(2), 251-256. Retrieved from http://proquest.umi.com/pqdweb?did=1287753501&sid=39&Fmt=2&clientId=1354&RQT=309&VName=PQD

Talmachoff, S. (1998). *Competitive advantage factor analysis of California silk firms: 1860-1930* (Doctoral dissertation). Available from ProQuest Dissertations and Theses database. (UMI No. 736783071)

Tandon, R. (1987). *Study of initial success for early investors in entrepreneurial new ventures* (Doctoral dissertation). Available from ProQuest Dissertations and Theses database. (UMI No. 753037071)

Taylor, D. & Smalling-Archer, J. (1994). *Up against the Wal-marts: How your business can prosper in the shadow of the retail giants,* New York, NY: American Management Association (Amacon).

Taylor, J. (1992). Factors and behaviors associated with successful technology substitution decisions in the high-turbulence environment (Doctoral dissertation).Available from ProQuest Dissertations and Theses database. (UMI No. 747440981)

Taylor J. M. (1997). *The network marketing game.* Salt Lake City, UT: King Alfred Press.

Thomas, R. D. (1991). *Dave's way.* New York, NY: G.P. Putman and Sons Press.

Thorne, J. (1992). *An analysis of the financial structure of the firm, managerial efficiency, and entrepreneurial risk-taking, given the existence of limited liability and moral hazard* (Doctoral dissertation). Available from ProQuest Dissertations and Theses database. (UMI No. 744698331)

Train, J. (1980). *The money masters: Nine great investors, their winning strategies and how you can apply them.* New York, NY: Harper & Row.

Trimble, V. H. (1990). *Sam Walton: The inside story of America's richest man.* New York, NY: Dutton.

Trump, D. & Schwartz, T. (1987). *Trump: The art of the deal.* New York, NY: Random House.

Turner, M. (2003). *Kmart's 10 deadly sins: How incompetence tainted an American icon.* Hoboken, NJ: John Wiley & Sons.

Tybout, A. & Sternthal, B. (2001). Brand positioning. In D. Iacobucci (Editor), *Kellogg on Marketing,* (pp. 11-28). New York, NY: John Wiley and Sons.

Unidimensional. (2009). In *Merriam-Webster Online Dictionary.* Retrieved from http://www.merriam-webster.com/dictionary/unidimensional

Vella, N. (2001). *Entrepreneurial attributes in malta* (Doctoral dissertation). Available from ProQuest Dissertations and Theses database. (UMI No. 726346441)

Vespers, K. (1989). *New venture strategies* (2nd ed.). Upper Saddle River, NJ: Prentice-Hall.

Vogt, P. (1993). *Dictionary of statistics and methodology.* Thousand Oaks, CA: Sage.

Volker, J. (2001). *The unexpected cost of entrepreneurship: An examination of investor penalties as reflected in P/E ratios* (Doctoral dissertation). Available from ProQuest Dissertations and Theses database. (UMI No. 728473861)

Vos, E. (1992). A conceptual framework for practical risk measurement in small businesses. *Journal of Small Business Management, 30*(3), 47. Retrieved from http://proquest.umi.com/pqdweb?did=591064&sid=40& Fmt=2& clientId=1354&RQT=309&VName=PQD

Walton, M. (1986). *The Deming management method.* New York, NY: Perigee Books.

Walton, S., & Huey, J. (1992). *Sam Walton: Made in America.* New York, NY: DoubleDay.

Wang, X. (2006). *Private equity, asset allocation and risk* (Doctoral dissertation). Available from ProQuest Dissertations and Theses database. (UMI No. 1251859131)

Watson, J. & Everett, J. (1996). Do small businesses have high failure rates? *Journal of Small Business Management, 34*(4), 45-62. Retrieved from http://proquest.umi.com/pqdweb?did=10501452&sid=41&Fmt=2&clie ntId=1354&RQT=309&VName=PQD

Watson, J. (2003). Failure rates for female-controlled businesses: Are they any different? *Journal of Small Business Management, 41*(3), 262. Retrieved from http://proquest.umi.com/pqdweb?did=356306811&Fmt=4&clientId=1 354&RQT=309&VName=PQD

White, G., Sondhi, A. & Fried, D. (1998). *The analysis and use of financial Statements* (2nd ed.). New York, NY: John Wiley & Sons.

Wiersma, W. & Jurs, S. (2005). *Research methods in education* (8th ed.). New York, NY: Allyn and Bacon.

Williams, J. (1978). A definition for the common-factor analysis model and the elimination of problems of factor score indeterminacy. *Psychometrika, 43*(1), 293-337.

Winakor, A., & Smith, R., (1935). Changes in financial structure of unsuccessful firms, *Bureau of Business Research* (Urbana, Ill.: University of Illinois Press, 1935).

Winfrey, F., & Budd, J. (1997). Reframing strategic risk. *S.A.M. Advanced Management Journal, 62*(4), 13-22. Retrieved from http://proquest.umi. com/pqdweb?did=25227985&sid=42&Fmt=2&clientId=1354&RQT=3 09&VName=PQD

Wu, X., & Knott, A. (2005, January). Entrepreneurial risk and market entry. *SBA Office Advocacy, 238*(3), 1-28.

Xu, H., & Ruef, M. (2004). The myth of the risk-tolerant entrepreneur. *Strategic Organization, 2*(4), 331-355. doi:10.1177/1476127004047617

Yamada, J. (2004). A multi-dimensional view of entrepreneurship: Towards a research agenda on organization emergence. *The Journal of Management Development, 23*(3/4), 289-320. Retrieved from http://proquest.umi.com /pqdweb?did=639767161&sid=43&Fmt=2&clientId=1354&RQT=309 &VName=PQD

Yrle, A., Hartman, S., & Yrle-Fryou, A. (2000). Economic factors: examining why small businesses fail. *Journal of Business and Entrepreneurship, 12*(3), 67-81 Retrieved from http://proquest.umi.com/pqdweb?did=139519763 1& sid=1&Fmt=7&clientId=1354& RQT=309&VName=PQD

Zacharakis, A. (1997). Entrepreneurial entry into foreign markets: A transaction cost perspective. *Entrepreneurship: Theory & Practice, 21*(3), 23-39.

Zahra, S. (2006). Entrepreneurial risk taking in family firms. *Family Business Review, 18*(1), 23-40. doi:10.1111/j.1741-6248.2007.00082.x

Zikmund, W. (2003a). *Business research methods* (7th ed.). New York, NY: Thomson-Southwestern.

Zikmund, W. (2003b). *Exploring market research* (8th ed.). New York, NY: Thomson-Southwestern.

Appendices I

Appendix A

Application for Institutional Review Board Approval Form
University of the Incarnate Word

(PLEASE TYPE INFORMATION)

1. Title of Study: A Model for Assessing Business Risk: A Quantitative Study on Entrepreneurial Risk Behavior of Small-To-Medium Enterprises

2. Principal Investigator (type name, telephone number, e-mail address and mailing address): D. Anthony Miles, (210)-362-0460; dmiles@uiwtx.edu or drderekx@yahoo.com; 4301 Broadway St, San Antonio, Texas, 78209

3. Co-Investigator; Faculty Supervisor; Thesis or Dissertation Chair: Dr. Judith Beauford

4. Division/Discipline: Education, Ph.D.

5. Research Category: a. _x__Exempt   b.____Expedited Review   c.____Full Board Review

6. Purpose of Study: (a) Test a researcher-developed instrument to measure entrepreneurial risk in nascent and incumbent small-to-medium business enterprises (SMEs); and (b) analyze differences in nascent and incumbent SMEs.

7. Number of Subjects:_250__ Controls:_____

8. Does this research involve any of the following:

	YES	NO
Inmates of penal institutions	____	_x_
Fetus in utero	____	_x_
Institutionalized mentally retarded	____	_x_
Viable fetus	____	_x_
Institutionalized mentally disabled	____	_x_
Nonviable fetus	____	_x_
Committed patients	____	_x_
Dead fetus	____	_x_
Mentally retarded outpatient	____	_x_
In vitro fertilization	____	_x_
Mentally disabled outpatient	____	_x_
Minors (under 18)	____	_x_
Pregnant women	____	_x_

For each "Yes", state what precautions you will use to obtain informed consent.

9. Duration of study: <u>12 months or 1 year</u>

10. How is information obtained? (Include instruments used): <u>online/web-based administration; personal administration; telephone; fax; mail.</u>

11. Confidentiality – Are data recorded anonymously? (__x__Yes _____No)

12. If #11 is answered "No", how will the study subjects' confidentiality be maintained?

13. Benefit of research: <u>Development of instrument to measure entrepreneurial risk; expand prior scope of research on entrepreneurial risk behavior of small-to-medium business enterprises.</u>

14. Possible risk to subjects: <u>none</u>

<u>IF CHANGE IN RESEARCH OCCURS THE BOARD MUST BE NOTIFIED BEFORE RESEARCH IS CONTINUED.</u>

Principal Investigator signature ___D. Anthony Miles_____

    Date___5/27/2009_____

Responsible Faculty signature ___Judith E. Beauford_____

    Date ___6/03/2009_____
(Required if student is Principal Investigator)

IRB Approval signature ___M. Risku_____

    Date___6/04/2009_____

Application # ___09-06-005_____

Appendix B

Protocol Submission Letter to University of the Incarnate Word IRB Committee

May 5, 2009

Dr. Michael Risku, Ph.D.
Chair, UIW Institutional Review Board

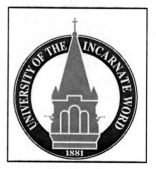

University of the Incarnate Word
4301 Broadway, San Antonio, Texas 78209

Dear Dr. Risku:

I am submitting the following research proposal for review by the University of the Incarnate Word Institutional Review Board, entitled, "A Model for Assessing Business Risk: A Quantitative Study on Entrepreneurial Risk Behavior of Small-to-Medium Enterprises."

Principal Investigator is <u>D. Anthony Miles</u>

The study will take place online; not at a physical location.

Brief Description of Study:

This study will test a researcher-designed instrument that measures entrepreneurial risk (ER) with nascent and incumbent small-to-medium business enterprises (SMEs). Building on key theoretical concepts grounded in economics literature, the Entrepreneurial Risk Assessment (ERA) instrument was developed for measuring the forces associated with small business risk. The defining ER forces identified from the economics literature are reflected in a 37-item survey.

Thank you for your attention and consideration. I will be happy to provide further information as requested *or you may contact me at 210-362-0460 and/or email at* dmiles@uiwtx.edu and drderekx@yahoo.com

Respectfully,

D. Anthony Miles

D. Anthony Miles, Principal Investigator
Doctoral Candidate, University of the Incarnate Word

Appendix C

Informed Consent Form

You are being asked to participate in a University of the Incarnate Word (UIW) research study on internal and external behavior of small and medium-sized businesses. You are being asked to complete a web-based survey to gather data concerning the knowledge you have of your business enterprise.

This survey is completely anonymous. There is no way to identify you as a participant. The only identification is by your ISP number.

You may choose not to participate in this study. There are no foreseeable risks, discomforts, or benefits to the participants in the study. However, this research will contribute to the body of knowledge regarding enterprise behavior. Additionally, the data collected will help us to learn more about endogenous and exogenous forces and their influence on small and medium business enterprises.

Your participation is voluntary and refusal to participate will involve no penalty or loss of benefits to which you are otherwise entitled.

The information provided will be kept confidential.

If you have any questions regarding this research please contact:

D. Anthony Miles, Doctoral Candidate
dmiles@uiwtx.edu or drderekx@yahoo.com
(210)-362-0460

Dr. Judith Beauford, Dissertation Committee Chair,
beauford@uiwtx.edu
(210)-829-3171

Dr. Kevin B. Vichcales, Dean of the School of Graduate Studies and Research
vichcale@uiwtx.edu
(210)-829-2759

By submission of this online form, you grant the permission to use your data for this study.

Thank you for your cooperation with this study.

Appendix D

Subject Matter Experts

	Expert	Background
1.	Dr. Dave Palmer, Ph.D.,	Executive Director of SCORE (Senior Corp of Retired Executives) and former Chief Financial Officer of Heritage Investigation and Security Incorporated;
2.	Estella Forhan	Executive Director of YWCA's Self-employment for Economic Development (SEED) Program and former business owner;
3.	Orestes Hubbard	Director of the Minority Business Development Center (MBDC) with University of Texas at San Antonio and former banker;
4.	David Baenziger	Senior Counselor, Small Business Development Center (SBDC) with University of Texas at San Antonio and former business owner;
5.	Mike Reyes	Senior Counselor, Small Business Development Center (SBDC) with University of Texas at San Antonio and former banker;
6.	Robert Ayala	Retired and former Small Business Administration (SBA) loan officer and Certified Public Accountant and Chief Executive Officer of Ayala Accounting Group, Incorporated;

7. Raul Rodriguez   Investment and international trade consulting firm in Mexico.

Subject Matter Expert Verification:
Dr. Dave Palmer, Ph.D.

May 18, 2009

Subject: Subject Matter Expert (SME) to ERA Instrument Developed by D. Anthony Miles, Doctoral Candidate, University of the Incarnate
To Whom It May Concern

I was asked to be to a participant as a small business Subject Matter Expert for D. Anthony Miles, doctoral candidate at the University of the Incarnate Word.

My role as a subject matter expert was to examine and evaluate his Entrepreneurial Risk Assessment (ERA) Instrument to be used for his dissertation study on small-to-medium enterprises (SMEs) in the Bexar County (San Antonio) area. In performing as a subject matter expert to this study, I have:

- Examined the ERA instrument, each risk variable and its significance to small-to-medium businesses enterprises (SMEs) in Bexar County-San Antonio.
- Provided my opinion on the importance of each risk variable and its impact on SMEs.
- After examining the ERA instrument to be used for this study, I have evaluated it and provided my subsequent comments, opinions, and recommendations.

If there are any other questions about my comments concerning the ERA instrument and its subject matter, please do not hesitate to contact me.

Thank you

Dave Palmer

Dr. Dave Palmer, Ph.D.
Senior of Retired Executives Corps (SCORE)
Office: (210) 403-5931
www.score.org

Subject Matter Expert Verification:
Mr. David Baenziger

May 21, 2009

Subject: Subject Matter Expert (SME) to ERA Instrument Developed by D. Anthony Miles, Doctoral Candidate, University of the Incarnate

To Whom It May Concern

I was asked to be to a participant as a small business Subject Matter Expert for D. Anthony Miles, doctoral candidate at the University of the Incarnate Word.

My role as a subject matter expert was to examine and evaluate his Entrepreneurial Risk Assessment (ERA) Instrument to be used for his dissertation study on small-to-medium enterprises (SMEs) in the Bexar County (San Antonio) area. In performing as a subject matter expert to this study, I have:

- Examined the ERA instrument, each risk variable and its significance to small-to-medium businesses enterprises (SMEs) in Bexar County-San Antonio.
- Provided my opinion on the importance of each risk variable and its impact on SMEs.
- After examining the ERA instrument to be used for this study, I have evaluated it and provided my subsequent comments, opinions, and recommendations.

If there are any other questions about my comments concerning the ERA instrument and its subject matter, please do not hesitate to contact me.

Thank you

David Baenziger

David Baenziger, Counseling Coordinator
UTSA-Small Business Development Center (SBDC)
Office: (210)- 458.2020

Subject Matter Expert Verification:
Mr. Orestes Hubbard

May 21, 2009

Subject: Subject Matter Expert (SME) to ERA Instrument Developed by D. Anthony Miles, Doctoral Candidate, University of the Incarnate

To Whom It May Concern

I was asked to be to a participant as a small business Subject Matter Expert for D. Anthony Miles, doctoral candidate at the University of the Incarnate Word.

My role as a subject matter expert was to examine and evaluate his Entrepreneurial Risk Assessment (ERA) Instrument to be used for his dissertation study on small-to-medium enterprises (SMEs) in the Bexar County (San Antonio) area. In performing as a subject matter expert to this study, I have:

- Examined the ERA instrument, each risk variable and its significance to small-to-medium businesses enterprises (SMEs) in Bexar County-San Antonio.
- Provided my opinion on the importance of each risk variable and its impact on SMEs.
- After examining the ERA instrument to be used for this study, I have evaluated it and provided my subsequent comments, opinions, and recommendations.

If there are any other questions about my comments concerning the ERA instrument and its subject matter, please do not hesitate to contact me.

Thank you

Orestes Hubbard

Orestes Hubbard, Director
UTSA - Minority Business Development Center (MBDC)
Office: (210)-458-2481

Subject Matter Expert Verification:
Mr. Mike Reyes

May 21, 2009

Subject: Subject Matter Expert (SME) to ERA Instrument Developed by D. Anthony Miles, Doctoral Candidate, University of the Incarnate

To Whom It May Concern

I was asked to be to a participant as a small business Subject Matter Expert for D. Anthony Miles, doctoral candidate at the University of the Incarnate Word.

My role as a subject matter expert was to examine and evaluate his Entrepreneurial Risk Assessment (ERA) Instrument to be used for his dissertation study on small-to-medium enterprises (SMEs) in the Bexar County (San Antonio) area. In performing as a subject matter expert to this study, I have:

- Examined the ERA instrument, each risk variable and its significance to small-to-medium businesses enterprises (SMEs) in Bexar County-San Antonio.
- Provided my opinion on the importance of each risk variable and its impact on SMEs.
- After examining the ERA instrument to be used for this study, I have evaluated it and provided my subsequent comments, opinions, and recommendations.

If there are any other questions about my comments concerning the ERA instrument and its subject matter, please do not hesitate to contact me.

Thank you

Mike Reyes

Mike Reyes, Senior Business Advisor
UTSA-Small Business Development Center (SBDC)
Office: (210)-458.2020

Subject Matter Expert Verification:
Ms. Estella Forhan

May 21, 2009

Subject: Subject Matter Expert (SME) to ERA Instrument Developed by D. Anthony Miles, Doctoral Candidate, University of the Incarnate
To Whom It May Concern

I was asked to be to a participant as a small business Subject Matter Expert for D. Anthony Miles, doctoral candidate at the University of the Incarnate Word.

My role as a subject matter expert was to examine and evaluate his Entrepreneurial Risk Assessment (ERA) Instrument to be used for his dissertation study on small-to-medium enterprises (SMEs) in the Bexar County (San Antonio) area. In performing as a subject matter expert to this study, I have:

- Examined the ERA instrument, each risk variable and its significance to small-to-medium businesses enterprises (SMEs) in Bexar County-San Antonio.
- Provided my opinion on the importance of each risk variable and its impact on SMEs.
- After examining the ERA instrument to be used for this study, I have evaluated it and provided my subsequent comments, opinions, and recommendations.

If there are any other questions about my comments concerning the ERA instrument and its subject matter, please do not hesitate to contact me.

Thank you

Estella Forhan

Estella Forhan, Director
YWCA's Self-employment for Economic Development (SEED) Program
Office: (210) 433-9922

Subject Matter Expert Verification:
Mr. Robert Ayala

May 18, 2009

Subject: Subject Matter Expert (SME) to ERA Instrument Developed by D. Anthony Miles, Doctoral Candidate, University of the Incarnate
To Whom It May Concern

I was asked to be to a participant as a small business Subject Matter Expert for D. Anthony Miles, doctoral candidate at the University of the Incarnate Word.

My role as a subject matter expert was to examine and evaluate his Entrepreneurial Risk Assessment (ERA) Instrument to be used for his dissertation study on small-to-medium enterprises (SMEs) in the Bexar County (San Antonio) area. In performing as a subject matter expert to this study, I have:

- Examined the ERA instrument, each risk variable and its significance to small-to-medium businesses enterprises (SMEs) in Bexar County-San Antonio.
- Provided my opinion on the importance of each risk variable and its impact on SMEs.
- After examining the ERA instrument to be used for this study, I have evaluated it and provided my subsequent comments, opinions, and recommendations.

If there are any other questions about my comments concerning the ERA instrument and its subject matter, please do not hesitate to contact me.

Thank you

Robert Ayala

Robert Ayala
Ayala Accounting Group
Office: (210) 393-3504

Appendix E

ERAS Survey Instrument-Paper Version

Researcher's Note:

I would like to thank you for your participation in this survey. I am completing my Ph.D. with a concentration in International Education and Entrepreneurship at the University of the Incarnate Word. I will be using this study in my final dissertation.

I am conducting a research study on characteristics of small businesses. I am not affiliated with any company or government organization. I am only interested in the study of firm behavior characteristics involved with your business enterprise.

Please note that your responses will be completely anonymous. I will not ask for your name or any other identifying information. I will collect this data from you and tabulate it with statistical software. If you request, I will send you a report of my findings.

Please complete every question and be as honest as possible.

Thank you for your participation in this study.

D. Anthony Miles, Doctoral Candidate
University of the Incarnate Word
Phone: (210) 362-0460   email: dmiles@uiwtx.edu or
drderekx@yahoo.com

(Please circle your answers).

1)   **What is your gender?**

   1 – Male   2 – Female

2)   **Which of the following best describes your current marital status?**

   1 – Single (never married)   4 – Widowed
   2 – Married   5 – Separated
   3 – Divorced

3)   **How many children are in the household?** (Please write in answer)

   _____

4)   **What is your current age?** (Please write in answer)

   _____

5)   **What is your highest level of education?**

   1 – Did not finish high school   4 – Bachelors
   2 – High school diploma   5 – Graduate degree
   3 – Some college   6 – Post graduate degree

6)   **What is your ethnicity?**

   1 – White (non-Hispanic)   4 – Asian, Pacific Islander
   2 – Black (non-Hispanic)   5 – Native American Indian
   3 – Hispanic   6 – Other

7)   **How much do you compensate yourself from your business annually?** (Please write in answer).

   _____

8) What is the industry or market sector of your business? (Choose one)

   1 – Agriculture   7 – Services
   2 – Communications   8 – Technology
   3 – Construction   9 – Transportation
   4 – Finance   10 – Wholesale trade
   5 – Manufacturing   11 – Other industry _____
   6 – Retail trade

9) How long have you owned your own business? (Please write answer).

10) How many years of experience do you have in the industry? (Please write in answer).

11) Is the business enterprise a franchise?

   1 – Yes   2 – No

12) How many employees do you have in your business? (Please write in answer).

13) Are you required to have any professional licenses (e.g. CPA, CFA, MD), to conduct business in your industry?

   1 – License   4 – Other
   2 – Certification   5 – None
   3 – Credential

14) The entity type of the business is a:

   1 – Corporation   4 – Sole proprietorship
   2 – Limited Liability Corporation (LLC) 5 – Other business
      or Limited Liability Partnership (LLP) Entity
   3 – Partnership _____

15) The capital (money) invested in your business to begin operations was: (Please write in answer).

16) Your business can continue to make a profit if you are not present in the business.

   Strongly   1   2   3   4   5   Strongly
   Disagree   Agree

17) The labor intensity involved to produce a product/service for your business is extremely high:

   Strongly   1   2   3   4   5   Strongly
   Disagree   Agree

18) The overhead costs in your business are extremely high:

   Strongly   1   2   3   4   5   Strongly
   Disagree   Agree

19) The business requires significant investment in equipment or technology.

   Strongly   1   2   3   4   5   Strongly
   Disagree   Agree

20) Your business uses internet technology extensively for your daily operations.

Strongly 1 2 3 4 5 Strongly
Disagree   Agree

21) The business has a team of experts for advice (e.g. attorney, banker, CPA, consultant, and insurance agent).

Strongly 1 2 3 4 5 Strongly
Disagree   Agree

22) The intellectual property of the business (business name, logo, etc.) has been registered with the U.S. Patent and Trademark Office.

Strongly 1 2 3 4 5 Strongly
Disagree   Agree

23) The customer pays the business for its product/service at purchase.

Strongly 1 2 3 4 5 Strongly
Disagree   Agree

24) The business enterprise maintains a high enough rate of customer transactions to achieve its profitability.

Strongly 1 2 3 4 5 Strongly
Disagree   Agree

25) Your customers primarily use credit to pay for the product/services.

Strongly 1 2 3 4 5 Strongly
Disagree   Agree

26) Your business has a line of credit with a bank or lending institution.

Strongly 1 2 3 4 5 Strongly
Disagree   Agree

27) The product/service is well established in the market.

Strongly 1 2 3 4 5 Strongly
Disagree   Agree

28) There are significant market entry barriers (e.g. technology, investment in equipment, patents, market share) for the business to begin operations.

Strongly 1 2 3 4 5 Strongly
Disagree   Agree

29) The market of the business has many competitors:

Strongly 1 2 3 4 5 Strongly
Disagree   Agree

30) The economic area of the business location is thriving and has growth:

Strongly 1 2 3 4 5 Strongly
Disagree   Agree

31) There are significant local, state, and federal government regulations (licensing, permits, certifications, etc.) required to do business in the market.

Strongly 1 2 3 4 5 Strongly
Disagree   Agree

32) The product/service of the business has a history of arousing negative attention from the media, law enforcement, schools or churches.

Strongly 1 2 3 4 5 Strongly
Disagree   Agree

33) Profits and operations can be strongly affected by extreme weather conditions in the business area.

Strongly 1 2 3 4 5 Strongly
Disagree   Agree

34) The profits of the business can be strongly affected by significantly high levels of crime in the business area.

Strongly 1 2 3 4 5 Strongly
Disagree   Agree

35) Profitability can be affected by an act of terrorism in the business location or economic area.

Strongly 1 2 3 4 5 Strongly
Disagree   Agree

36) The business is free to adjust its pricing with a rise in energy costs (e.g. fuel, gas, oil) without constraints to its profitability.

Strongly 1 2 3 4 5 Strongly
Disagree   Agree

37) The business can sustain its profits despite the entry of global and dominant competitors (e.g. Wal-Mart, McDonald's) into the local market.

Strongly 1 2 3 4 5 Strongly
Disagree   Agree

Appendices II

Appendix A

Pilot Study and Field Testing Results:
Beta Version of ERAS instrument

To determine the appropriate question content, a pilot study of a beta version of the ERAS instrument was conducted prior to the formal research study. As a result of this investigation, the ERAS instrument for this research study was developed. The instrument was developed from the economics literature. The literature from economics, management, marketing, finance and entrepreneurship established the priori dimensions of the (1) personal characteristics; (2) intangible operations; (3) enterprise operations; (4) market climate; and (5) business environment. The pilot study was conducted with participants who possessed the matching similarities and characteristics of the participants in sample of the formal study.

Babbie (1973) advises that a pilot study analysis should be carried out with all the vigor and imagination intended for the final analysis; the results of the pilot study should be essentially the same as those of the final survey. The conventional wisdom concerning an adequate number of participants for a pilot study varies among the scholars. Keppel (1982) made the argument that an adequate pilot study to determine the reliability of the instrument can have roughly as little as 16 participants. Long, Convey and Chwalek (1985) have argued that probably 30 or more individuals would be desirable to field test an instrument. On the other hand, Fowler (1995) argued that when a survey instrument is in near final form, experienced field researchers normally conduct 15-35 interviews with people similar to those who will be participants in the planned survey. However, the threat of this practical approach with pilot studies sometimes tend to give unreliable results, largely due to (a) the small numbers of subjects tested; and (b) may often provide questionable usefulness in designing the major study (Keppel, 1982; Anderson, Sweeny & Williams, 1990; Fowler, 1998). The pilot study for the beta version of the ERAS had more than exceeded the advised minimum number (15-35) of participants for a pilot. The pilot study for the beta ERAS consisted of 201 solicited participants from the Bexar County (San Antonio Metropolitan) area in 2008.

The pilot study for the beta ERAS instrument was based on a convenience sample from two local chambers of commerce directories of individuals who owned businesses, based upon availability. The pilot study consisted of 201 solicited participants from the Bexar County and San Antonio Metropolitan area. This represented a 32% response rate over a period of one year.

The beta version of the ERAS instrument which measured entrepreneurial risk orientation (ERO) frequency was based on a 31-item (forced response) scale. The beta version of the ERAS consisted of five subscales. Items were developed from the review of the literature, economics literature and amended with input from business practitioners (see Table 21). A Cronbach's alpha coefficient was computed to determine the internal consistency (reliability) of the ERAS instrument. The rationale for computing Cronbach's alpha is to provide evidence of the reliability of the values obtained from the instrument and to identify individual items that might affect the overall reliability of the instrument (Kerlinger, 1985). The Cronbach's alpha coefficient for the 31 items in the pilot study was equal to (.80) measure of internal consistency. The recommended minimum is .70; this study exceeded this.

Results of Pilot Study: Demographics

The data compiled from the surveys was entered in SPSS 17.0 for Windows. The researcher used descriptive statistics when compiling data on the demographics. The sample of the pilot study consisted of 201 small-to-medium business enterprises (SMEs).

The descriptive statistics of the pilot sample were as follows: (a) gender - 32.8% were male SME owners and 67.2% were female SME owners; (b) marital status - 63.2% of SME owners were married; (c) age - 33.8% of SME owners were ages 47-57; (d) education level - 32.8% of SME possessed a baccalaureate degree; (e) ethnicity - 36.3% of SME owners were Hispanic; (f) gross personal income - 19.9% of SME owners grossed between $60K to $100K and; and (g) time length of business ownership - 41.8% of SME owners owned their business less than one year. Overall, the pilot sample had considerably more female SME owner respondents than their male counterparts. Review the following tables:

Table 21. Pilot Study Demographics of Gender and Marital Status

Variables	Frequency	Percent
Gender		
Males	66	32.8%
Females	135	67.2%
Marital Status		
Single	28	13.9%
Married	127	63.9%
Divorced	30	14.9%
Widowed	9	4.5%
Separated	7	3.5%

($N = 201$)

Table 22. Pilot Study Demographics of Age and Education Level

Variables	Frequency	Percent
Age		
18 – 24	6	3.0%
25 – 35	32	15.9%
36 – 46	59	29.4%
47 – 57	68	33.8%
57 and over	36	17.9%
Education Level		
Did not finish high school	8	4.0%
High school Diploma	17	8.5%
Some college	66	32.8%
Bachelors degree	60	29.9%
Graduate degree	32	15.9%
Post-graduate degree or higher	18	9.0%

($N = 201$)

Table 23. Pilot Study Demographics of Ethnicity, Gross Income Generated from Business and Time Length of Owning Business

Variables	Frequency	Percent
Ethnicity		
White	62	30.8%
Black (non-Hispanic)	54	26.9%
Hispanic	73	36.3%
Asian (Pacific Islander)	2	1.0%
Native American Indian	4	2.0%
Other	6	3.0%
Gross Income Generated from Business		
Under $10,000	23	11.4%
$10,000 to $25,000	33	16.4%
$25,001 to $40,000	35	17.4%
$40,001 to $60,000	40	19.9%
$60,000 to $100,000	39	19.4%
Over $100,000	31	15.4%
Time Length of Owning Business		
Less than 1 year	84	41.85
1 to 3 years	39	19.4%
4 years or more	78	38.8%

($N = 201$)

Factor Analysis Used in the Pilot Study

For the pilot study, a principal component factor analysis was performed on the beta version of ERAS. The piloted study factor analysis was performed with SAS ® (Statistical Analysis System) Version 9.1 software. Nine factors were extracted with a varimax rotation. The pilot study's eigenvalues and loadings of the variables and covariance are shown on Table 24 and Table 25. The factor coefficient loadings greater than .3 are indicated in bold text.

Benchmark for a Factor Analysis

As a benchmark in terms of factor loadings, typically, researchers consider variables with factor loadings coefficients of at least .3 in absolute value as loading on eigenvector; thus as worthy of consideration in the interpretation of the meaning of the eigenvector. Others have argued that the practice of only considering factor coefficients loadings of greater than .3 ignores the number of observations in the sample (Rummel, 1970; Long, 1985; Bryant & Yarnold, 2008). It is a common practice for researchers conducting a factor analysis to consider only factor loadings > .3 (see Tables 24 and 25).

Table 24. Pilot Study Results of Eigenvalues, Percentages of Variance, and Cumulative Percentages for Beta Version of ERAS Instrument (N = 201)

Factor	Eigenvalues	% of Variance	% of Cumulative
1	3.057	13.290	13.290
2	2.396	10.415	23.706
3	1.870	8.130	31.836
4	1.796	7.807	39.643
5	1.420	6.175	45.817
6	1.266	5.505	51.322
7	1.130	4.912	56.234
8	1.113	4.841	61.075
9	1.056	4.590	65.666

Note. Extraction Method: Principal Component Analysis

Table 25. Pilot Study Factor Analysis Results of 22-item and 9-Factor Solution Loadings with Beta ERAS Risk Variables ($N = 201$)

Items	F1	F2	F3	F4	F5	F6	F7	F8	F9
COMPETITIVE RISK	**.973**	.014	.078	-.045	.027	.087	.021	-.026	.043
INDUSTRY TYPE	**.971**	.020	.052	-.088	.020	.092	.037	.012	.066
SECURITY RISK	.039	**.808**	.098	.103	.055	-.048	.053	-.113	-.076
TERRORISM RISK	.032	**.802**	-.084	-.041	.045	.152	-.117	.142	-.010
ENVIRONMENT RISK	-.010	**.544**	.240	-.037	.187	.150	.232	-.049	.205
GOVERNMENT	.169	.039	**.802**	.124	-.030	-.112	.034	.068	.115
REGULATION RISK	-.053	.056	**.714**	-.012	.295	.017	-.027	.164	-.091
MARKET ENTRY RISK	.061	.103	**.500**	**.493**	-.027	.026	-.059	-.266	-.152
CAPITAL INVESTMENT RISK	-.043	-.039	.075	**.773**	.054	-.051	-.016	.038	-.013
SOCIAL RISK	-.089	.242	.185	**.614**	-.014	.039	.250	**.364**	**.304**
CUSTOMER TURNOVER RISK	.019	.029	.029	**-.456**	-.238	.456	-.079	**.314**	.042
MARKET POTENTIAL RISK	-.250	-.219	-.281	**.319**	-.014	-.118	.154	-.104	.182
DISECONOMIES OF SCALE	.094	.147	.060	-.041	**.788**	.037	.052	.065	-.091
GLOBALIZATON RISK	-.122	-.014	.183	.080	**.660**	.130	.048	-.067	**.377**
INTELLECTUAL CAPITAL RISK	.138	.065	-.015	.066	.061	**.806**	.028	-.059	-.129
TIME INTENSIVENESS RISK	.073	.184	-.080	-.182	.112	**.537**	.152	.130	.169
EXPERTISE INDUSTRY RISK	-.061	.011	-.046	.057	.065	.064	**.808**	.136	-.099
BUSINESS ENTITY RISK	.120	.040	.099	-.172	-.112	-.057	**.550**	**-.341**	-.053
PROTECTION DEVICES RISK	.111	.031	-.121	-.016	.216	.338	**.536**	**-.434**	.107

Items	F1	F2	F3	F4	F5	F6	F7	F8	F9
VELOCITY OF PROFIT RISK	.017	-.037	.134	-.046	.080	.121	-.070	**.733**	-.114
INFLATION ENERGY RISK	.193	.236	-.048	.106	**.446**	**-.356**	.058	**.480**	.027
BUSINESS CLIMATE RISK	.106	.050	.044	-.037	.111	.029	-.124	-.093	**.796**
LABOR RISK	.014	.214	.227	.189	**.343**	.296	-.233	.048	**-.458**

Note. Extraction Method: Principal Component Factor Analysis.
Rotation Method: Varimax with Kaiser Normalization.
Rotation converged in 10 iterations. Loadings >.3 are in bold text.

The principal factors extraction with a varimax rotation was performed through SAS FACTOR on 22 items from the beta version of ERAS for a sample of 201 SMEs. Principal components extraction was used prior to principal factors extraction to estimate number of factors, presence of outliers and factorability of the correlation matrices. Nine factors were extracted (see Table 25). As indicated by ERAS, all factors were internally consistent and well defined by the variables. The factor loadings of variables and communalities and percents of variance and covariance are shown. Variables are ordered and grouped by size of factor loadings to facilitate interpretation. Factor loadings .3 and above are in bold text.

Appendix B

ERAS Beta Version - Entrepreneur Survey Instrument

Section 1: Demographic Data (please circle answers)

1) **What is your gender?**
   1 - Male   2 - Female

2) **Which of the following best describes your current marital status?**
   1 – Single (never married)
   2 – Married
   3 – Divorced
   4 – Widowed
   5 – Separated

3) **What is your current age?**
   1 – (18 to 24)
   2 – (25 to 35)
   3 – (36 to 46)
   4 – (47 to 57)
   5 – (57 and over)

4) **What is your highest level of education?**
   1 - Did not finish high school
   2 - High school diploma
   3 - Some college
   4 - Bachelors
   5 - Graduate degree
   6 - Post graduate degree and higher

5) **What is your ethnicity?**
   1 - White
   2 - Black (non-Hispanic)
   3 - Hispanic
   4 – Asian (Pacific Islander)
   5 - Native American Indian
   6 - Other

Researcher's Note:

I would like to thank you for your participation in this survey. I am completing my Ph.D. with a concentration in International Education and Entrepreneurship (I.E. & E.) at the University of the Incarnate Word. I will be using this study as my final dissertation.

I am conducting a research study on entrepreneurial risk with new and existing businesses. Let me emphasize that I am not affiliated with any companies or government organizations. I am interested in the study of risk involved with your business enterprise.

Please note that all this information is completely anonymous. I will not ask for your name or any other identifying information. I will collect this data from you and tabulate it with statistical software. I will send you a report with my findings if you are interested. Please provide me with your contact information (first and last name initials, address information or email address).

Please complete every question and be as honest as possible.

Thank you for your participation in this study.

D. Anthony Miles, Doctoral Candidate
University of the Incarnate Word
Phone: 362-0460 email: drderelx@yahoo.com

1) **What is your business entity type?**
   1 - Corporation (S or C)
   2 - Limited Liability Corporation (LLC) or Partnership (LLP)
   3 – Neutral; not sure
   4 - Partnership
   5 - Sole proprietorship

2) **How much money has been or was needed for investment in your business or enterprise to begin operations?**
   1 - 0 to $50,000
   2 - $50,001 to $100,000
   3 - $100,001 to $500,000
   4 - $500,001 to $900,000
   5 - $900,001 and over

3) **Can the business or enterprise continue to make a profit if you are not present in the business?**
   1 - Can operate without your presence.
   2 - Can partially operate without your presence.
   3 – Neutral; not sure
   4 - Cannot operate partially without your presence.
   5 - Cannot operate without your presence.

4) **How much labor costs are involved in your business or enterprise to produce a product/service for profit?**
   1 - Not labor intensive to produce the product or service.
   2 - Somewhat labor intensive to produce a product or service.
   3 – Neutral; not sure
   4 - Highly labor intensive to produce a product or service.
   5 - Extremely labor intensive to produce a product or service.

6) **What was your approximate personal gross income last year?**
   1 – Under $10,000
   2 - $10,000 - $25, 0000
   3 - $25,001 - $40,000
   4 - $40,001 - $60,000
   5 - $60,001 - $100,000
   6 – Over $100,000

7) **How long have you owned your own business?**
   1 – (Less than 1 year)
   2 – (1 to 3 years)
   3 – (4 years or more)

Section 2: Entrepreneur Survey Instrument
(please circle answers)

5) **How much experience do you have in the industry or market sector of the business?**
   1 – (20 years or more of experience)
   2 – (11 to 20 years of experience)
   3 – (6 to 10 years of experience)
   4 – (2 to 5 years of experience)
   5 – (0 to 1 year of experience)

6) Does your business require significant investment in equipment or systems for its operations to be profitable?
1 - No investment
2 – Somewhat minimal investment
3 - Neutral
4 - High investment
5 - Extremely high investment

7) Can your product or service be sold over the Internet?
1 - Extremely high potential for being sold over the Internet.
2 - High potential for being sold over the Internet.
3 – Neutral; not sure
4 – Low potential of being sold over the Internet.
5 – Extremely low potential of being sold over the Internet.

8) Does the business have a team of experts for advice (i.e. attorney, banker, CPA, and insurance agent)?
1 - Attorney, banker, CPA and insurance agent
2 - Attorney, banker, CPA.
3 – Neutral; not sure
4 – No attorney, no CPA, but banker.
5 – None

9) Is the business name or logo trademarked with the U.S. Patent and Trademark Office?
1 – Business name and logo are trademarked.
2 – Somewhat: name and logo are both pending trademarks.
3 – Neutral
4 – Have not trademarked business name, but okay with logo.
5 – Have not trademarked both business name and logo.

10) How long does it take for the business to be paid for the product or services from the customer (i.e. credit or invoicing)?
1 - Paid immediately
2 - A day or more than 24 hours
3 – Neutral; not sure
4 - A week or more
5 – A month or more (invoicing).

11) How fast does the business turnover customers through the operation per day?
1 – (20 or more customers per day).
2 – (15 or customers or less per day).
3 – (Neutral; not sure)
4 – (10 or less customers per day).
5 – (5 or less customers per day).

12) Is your product or service completely new or an existing one?
1 - Product/service has existed for 6 years or more.
2 - Product/service has existed for 3 to 5 years.
3 - Not sure; neutral
4 - Product/service is nearly new; 2 or more years in existence.
5 - New product/service; none exist on the market.

13) Are there any significant market entry barriers (i.e. significant investment in equipment or licensing and certifications)?
1 - Highly unlikely
2 - Unlikely
3 - Not sure; neutral
4 - Likely
5 - Highly likely

14) Can your business maintain its operations during severe extreme weather conditions (i.e. high rains, extreme temperatures, floods, hurricanes, tornados, earthquakes, etc)?

1 – No significant changes in operations
2 – Very few significant changes in operations
3 - Not sure; neutral
4 - High significant changes in operations
5 - Extremely high significant changes in operations

15) Can the profits of your business be strongly affected by significant levels of crime in the business location?

1 - No significant effect on profits
2 - Very few significant effects on profits
3 - Not sure; neutral
4 - High significant effect on profits
5 - Extremely high significant effect on profits

16) Can the profits of your business be affected by an act of terrorism in the business location and economic area?

1 - No significant effect on profits
2 - Very few significant effects on profits
3 - Not sure; neutral
4 - High significant effect on profits
5 - Extremely high significant effect on profits

17) Is your business free to adjust its pricing with an increase in inflation or rise in energy costs (i.e. gas, oil) without constraints to maintain its profits?

1 - Can adjust pricing freely.
2 - Can adjust pricing with some constraints to maintain profits.
3 - Not sure; neutral
4 - Cannot adjust pricing with some constraints to maintain profits.
5 - Cannot adjust pricing freely.

18) How many (local) competitors do you have in your market?

1 – (0 to 4 competitors)
2 – (5 to 10 competitors)
3 – (Not sure; neutral)
4 – (11 to 20 competitors)
5 – (21 or more competitors)

19) What is the economic condition concerning the location of your business (i.e. is the economic area thriving; high development or declining; low development)?

1 - Highly thriving economic area.
2 - Somewhat thriving economic area.
3 - Not sure; neutral
4 - Somewhat declining economic area.
5 - Highly declining economic area.

20) Are there significant local, state, or federal government regulations (licensing, permits, certifications etc.) required for you to do business in your market?

1 - No significant government regulations.
2 - Very few governmental regulations.
3 - Not sure; neutral
4 - High significant government regulations.
5 - Extremely high significant government regulations.

21) Does your product or service have a history of arousing negative attention from the media, law enforcement, schools or churches?

1 - No significant negative attention
2 – Some significant negative attention
3 - Not sure; neutral
4 - High significance of negative attention.
5 - Extremely high significance of negative attention

**22) Can your business be expanded globally to handle transna-
tional competitors?**

    1 - Can be expanded globally.

    2 - Can be expanded globally with some modifications to
    product /service.

    3 - Not sure; neutral

    4 - Cannot be expanded globally even with some modifica-
    tions to the

        product or service.

    5 - Cannot be expanded globally.

Index

Dr. D. Anthony Miles is CEO and founder of Miles Development Industries Corporation®, a venture consulting practice and venture capital acquisition firm. Miles is a leading expert in the areas of entrepreneurial risk, entrepreneurship, and business model development. He has over 20 years' experience in the private sector. He has held positions with fortune 500 companies such as PAC Incorporated, Wells Fargo Bank, Reliance Acceptance Corporations, CitiFinancial, (a subsidiary of Citigroup Bank), and H.E.B. Grocery Store Chain. He has consulted several start-up ventures and small businesses on business risk, business plans, entity formation, and market research. He consulted and developed a business plan and strategic plan for Brooks City-Base, a former military base that was under Base Realignment Closure (BRAC) in San Antonio, Texas. He conducted research on minority contract awards trends with the City of San Antonio Government's Economic Development Department. He has conducted market research on the feasibility of bringing a major franchise to Alamo Colleges-Palo Alto College in San Antonio, Texas. He is also an adjunct professor with the College of Business at Texas A&M University-San Antonio. Prior he taught business courses as a visiting professor at Centro Universitario-Incarnate Word (CIW) in Mexico City, Mexico. He has taught courses in management, marketing, market research, entrepreneurship, small business management, and finance. His areas of research specialty are in entrepreneurship, small business, management, venture capital, organizational behavior, marketing, economic development, and general business.

CPSIA information can be obtained at www.ICGtesting.com
Printed in the USA
LVOW06s0343261215

467896LV00006B/29/P